So Dear to My Heart

So Dear to My Heart

MEMORIES OF A GENTLER TIME

Jane Goyer

1817

HARPER & ROW, PUBLISHERS, New York
Grand Rapids, Philadelphia, St. Louis, San Francisco
London, Singapore, Sydney, Tokyo, Toronto

The following essays first appeared in the *Worcester* (Mass.) *Senior Advocate*: "Thanksgiving on the Farm," "Papa's Garden," "Welcome, Peddlers," "When Mama's Ship Comes In," "Headphones and Belly Laughs," "That Old Gypsy Mystique," "Summers of Old," "Too Fat to Be an Angel," "Those Fabulous Toys of My Childhood," "Christmas Shopping with Great-Aunt Amanda," "When the Drummers Came to Town," "Mother's Infatuation with Honest Abe," "The Thanksgiving That Almost Wasn't," "Recalling the Nickelodeon," "Valentine Memory from 1916," "Sweet Songs of Yesteryear," and "Never Wipe Your Nose on Your Coat Sleeve."

"A World I Never Made" appeared in the *New York Times*. © 1989 by The New York Times Company. Reprinted by permission.

FIRST EDITION

Designer: Helene Berinsky

Library of Congress Cataloging-in-Publication Data
Goyer, Jane, 1894–
   So dear to my heart : memories of a gentler time/Jane Goyer.—
1st ed.
      p.   cm.
   ISBN 0-06-016225-2
   1. Goyer, Jane, 1894– —Childhood and youth.   2. Worcester
(Mass.)—Social life and customs.   3. Worcester (Mass.)—Biography.
4. City and town life—Massachusetts—Worcester—History—20th
century.   I. Title.
F74.W9G68   1990
974.4'3—dc20
[B]   89-45658

90 91 92 93 94 AT/HC 10 9 8 7 6 5 4 3 2 1

Contents

Acknowledgments

I wish to thank my loving family for their help and encouragement and all my good friends at Colony Retirement Homes, whose calls and comments helped so much. Also Sondra of the *Worcester Senior Advocate,* who did most of the work, beyond the writing.

And Olive, an old writing friend, my most ardent fan. Also the Clearwater Branch of Pen Women International, and Mary-Lou, one of its board members, who urged me on when I was ready to give up. And last, but not least, my agent, Freya Manston, who was so helpful, and my publishers, who have been so kind and thoughtful.

So Dear to My Heart

Mama's Big Day

EVERYTHING ABOUT OUR FAMILY WAS BIG. WE WERE nine when alone. Papa and Mama and seven children. From Lewis, eighteen years, to baby Ted, six months. And Grandma Goodness, when it was her turn to visit, and sometimes Grandpa too. And always a big collie dog, and at least two cats, and kittens. And often other pets, a rabbit, one or two hamsters, or even a tiny alligator. And we lived in a big house. Seven rooms, a big bathroom, an enormous attic, and a big cement-floor basement. It was a new house, and very modern for the times. It had a big guest room with a washbowl, set tubs in the basement, a white enamel double sink in the kitchen, and hot and cold water. And it was steam heated. There were twelve faucets in the house. It was quite luxurious.

But it was a rented house, fifteen dollars a month, and Mama thought that was a terrible price to pay. Only Papa was bringing in money. But, with our big family, it was all we could get. And we got that only because Papa knew a friend of the owner. We had been living before that in a four-room cottage, and there was no room for two new babies.

Mama had one great desire, and that was to have a home of our own. She saved every penny, every nickel, every dime, that she possibly could. When a big double loaf of bread went from five cents to seven cents, she started baking her own. When a bar of laundry soap went from five cents to six, she saved her fat scraps, and made her own soft soap. She got soup bones at the market, free, and made us huge kettles of soup. She got fish heads from the fish man, free, and made delicious chowder with it. She made our tooth powder with salt, soda, and borax. She patched, she darned, she made over from one child to the next oldest. She was up and doing at sunrise, and went to bed at seven o'clock on winter evenings. Papa stayed up with us children until nine o'clock, playing cards with us, or checkers, or dominoes. At nine-thirty, the house was quiet, everyone in bed.

There was a nice yard, and we had one of those two-seated wooden swings in it. On summer evenings, Mama would stay up a little later. And after we children had gone upstairs to bed, she would sit out in the swing with Papa. I would sometimes watch them from my little back bedroom window. They would talk and talk, and sometimes Mama would pat Papa's knee. And sometimes Papa would lean over and pat Mama's cheek. I never saw them embrace, but they had other ways of showing their affection for each other. Mama's name was Roseanne. She hated to be called Rosie. But Papa was a great tease, and often he did call her that. They usually called each other *Vieux* and *Vieille*. In English this means only "Old Man" and "Old Lady." But in French it is a term of endearment. No man would call his wife *Vieille* unless he was very fond of her.

Papa had a pet name for each of us. I was "Bounce" because of my curly hair — I reminded him of a little curly dog we had once with that name. My brother Wilfred was "Peck" after the popular book *Peck's Bad Boy*. We couldn't pronounce Wilfred, so for years he was "Fa-fa Peck." My sister Rose was quite dark of complexion, and Papa called her "Noirette," which we could not pronounce, so she was "Waette." Papa spoke beautiful French, so pure that the Canadians could not understand him. And he was rather a dandy, with a little twisted black mustache.

On this particular warm spring day in 1904, Mama, dressed in her best long black skirt and white shirtwaist, told us that she must go out for a while. She had left a kettle of soup for us on the stove. We must stay in, take good care of the babies, be good, and she would try not to be too long. But she was gone almost all day. Papa was back home from work when she came back. She was in very high spirits, very flushed and excited. She took off her hat with the little red rose on it, then held her arms out to us.

"Gather round, dear children, and Vieux, for I have wonderful news for you. Very wonderful news. You'll never believe it! I've bought us a house. A home of our own. It's not a new house like this, but it is a good house, a big house. Four big bedrooms. You, Jen, won't have to share your bedroom with Grandma. The babies will have a little nursery. There is a big yard, bigger than this one. And it is all fenced in. You can play ball, croquet, have swings. And there is a big cherry tree, apple trees, and a grapevine. Oh! It is going to be Paradise! No landlord to tell us what we can or cannot do. And no more fifteen dollars a month."

Then she told us all about it. She had read in the paper about an auction, a house to be sold for unpaid taxes. The house went for $2,000. She was the highest bidder. She had only $1,800, she said, but planned to borrow the rest. "I won't need to, though," she said, "as the bank is giving me a mortgage, because it is such a good, solid house." And she added, "Our credit is good. We don't owe anyone."

Papa went to her, and put his arms on her shoulders. "How can I believe this woman of mine?" Then, "Children, look at your mother, and realize—there is no one else like her." He wanted to celebrate. So he got out the freezer and made ice cream. And Mama got out the cookie jar. We were all very excited.

But I was not so very happy over this surprise. I loved the big attic of the rented house. My toys and books were all there. I loved my little playmates who lived nearby, and I loved my teacher, Miss Burns. No, I could not feel too happy.

And when I first saw the new home (for us), I was

appalled. Instead of twelve faucets, there was one faucet over a black iron kitchen sink. No bathroom, only a three-holer in a shed attached to the kitchen. No hot water. A dirt-floor cellar. An unfinished attic. It was cold, for there was no heat. We bought a potbellied stove for the middle room, which we'd use as a sitting room, as the parlor would be kept closed in the winter.

We moved in on a cold, windy day. The oldest baby, one and a half years old, caught cold, and then pneumonia. The barrels stayed unopened. Mama spent all her time with him, and I cared for the littlest one. But she saved him, and once he was well, she settled down quickly, and loved the new home, never missing the hot water and other luxuries, singing all day in her lovely, sweet, thin voice. It wasn't very long before we had some of our luxuries back. Her first project was to raze the three-holer shed and put in a bathroom. Then, a white double enamel sink, and cabinets. And hot water. And every room papered over with bright cheerful paper.

I had to admit that there were some nice things about this old house. The windows were small-paned, eight over eight panes. The front door was lovely (after Papa painted it), with a fan-shaped pane at the top. In the front hall was a beautiful little stained-glass window. The front stairs were curved and the banister posts carved. The second year, Papa installed a hot-air furnace, and grates in the ceiling. The first time he fired it, we ran to our rooms to wait for the heat to come up. "It's coming!" we shouted. "It's getting warm!" That was a gala day.

The furnace was fired only on weekends. Then the parlor was opened. Mama would sit in the warm parlor in her favorite rocking chair. Rock, smile, and meditate. We'd let her be. She needed a time alone. On my eleventh birthday, she bought me a used piano, an Emerson. And I took lessons, at fifty cents a lesson. That was a great sacrifice for Mama. So I started baby-sitting for the neighbors for a dime an hour. But I had to kill flies, wash diapers, and feed babies to earn that much. The first time I took two dimes home to Mama, she kissed me, and said, "God will give you a talent, I know it. Because you are such a good help to me." But though I enjoyed playing the piano, I knew I would never be a talented player. I hated to practice. I would much rather read or write.

Then Mama decided to have little sister Bea take lessons, but she too, hated to practice. Well, Mama decided that the piano purchase would not be wasted. So she took our exercise books, and each evening, after the household work was done, she studied them, and plunked at the piano. In less than three months, she could play much better than we could. And she loved it.

There was no big rent to pay now, and Lewis, the oldest, was working. A little more money was coming in. Mama made one improvement after another. A lovely, colorful, and thick Brussels carpeting was put down on the parlor floor. Every room had been painted over and papered with pretty wallpaper. We did all the work ourselves. She made lovely, frilly, ruffled curtains and bedspread of pink and white rosebuds for my little bedroom.

She made apple pies and sauce and juice with the apples from the apple trees, cherry pies and preserves from the big cherry tree, grape jelly and jams and even a little wine for Grandpa from the grapevine. The big cabinet in the cellar was full of bottles, jars, and glasses, bright with fruit. We were poor, but we felt wealthy.

We had the first gaslights in the neighborhood. We had the first telephone. We had the first washing machine, worked with a hand crank. We were only a few steps from the school, and we got to know all the teachers. For Mama was always willing to loan them things they needed, or to let them use the telephone.

I was very happy here now. We had circuses in our big backyard using all the animals in the neighborhood as wild beasts. We had plays, pageants, and art shows. We had our two-seated wooden swing, on a big, thick, rope hung from a heavy branch of the apple tree. The littlest ones were safe in the fenced-in yard.

We all lived in that house until we were married. No one ever thought of leaving. After we had lived there for a few years, we had a big housewarming. All our friends and neighbors came. We hung Japanese lanterns all around the yard, and decorated the house with autumn leaves. We had a small band playing, and the young people danced on the lawn. We set a long table in the kitchen, and piled it with finger foods and lots of homemade drinks. And a big punch bowl of iced lemonade with a bit of wine. It was a lovely party. And Mama and Papa were given a beautiful oak sideboard for the middle room, which we now used as a dining room.

The next day Papa came in with a large flat package, wrapped in blue paper with a great blue bow. Mama had another pet name she often used for Papa. "*Bonhomme,*" she said, "what do you have there?" Papa twisted his mustache. "I want to give you my own personal gift. Something you've been admiring for a long time." He laid it on the table, and Mama unwrapped it. It was a popular painting of the day, *A Yard of Roses.* Very colorful, very lovely, in a golden frame. Tears filled Mama's eyes. "Oh!" she cried. "This is the last thing I have wished for, for the parlor." She had been selling and buying Larkin products to furnish our parlor with lovely mahogany pieces. Love seat, gate-leg table, rocking chair, and a Tiffany lamp. Now, we hung the long painting, *Yard of Roses,* over the piano. It was perfect, the colors coordinating with the pretty colors in the carpeting. Mama sat in her rocker and admired, her eyes still full of tears.

I've kept that vision with me all through the years.

Memory Street

Now, after eighty-eight years, I can visualize the street where I lived my childhood years with no effort at all. In my mind I can walk to the north end of the street, cross over, and walk back down the street to our house. And I can name every family that lived in those houses and describe them. I can remember how many children lived in each one, and their names. I can tell you what the father did for a living. I knew them all that well.

Most of the children were born Americans, but many of their parents were not. But we were all learning to be good Americans. To grow up on this street was to live in a pure democracy. We were as unconscious of class as it was possible to be. On that block (we called it the neighborhood, not the block) were storekeepers, factory hands, waiters and waitresses, bartenders, mill hands, a saloon owner, a doctor, and a lawyer.

Mama's very best friend lived right across the road from us. She and James, her husband, were not related to us at all, but we called them Aunt Mag and Uncle Jim. To Mama she was just "Mag." She was very fat. Very fat and soft. I doubt that she ever wore a corset. She just overflowed. But she had a very sweet face, skin as pink as a rose petal, lovely china-blue eyes, and hair like spun gold, which she wore brushed back and piled up high on her head.

Aunt Mag was born in Ireland, came over to work as a servant girl, but met Uncle Jim and married him soon afterwards. Uncle Jim was not well, suffering from some malady, and could work only a few days a week to keep the household going. Aunt Mag had a lovely sweet voice, and knew all the old Irish songs. She played the piano and organ very well. When Uncle Jim felt well enough, he sang with her, and when they spent an evening in our parlor entertaining us, it was a wonderful evening for us. They had an Edison phonograph, and sometimes they would bring that over and play all their records for us. No television ever gave me as much joy as those musical evenings did.

After Uncle Jim died, Aunt Mag grieved, and we missed her. One day she called, early in the morning, to tell Mama that a Mr. S., a "round the corner" neighbor, a widower, had been calling on her, and wanted to marry her. "He is a good man," she said, "and I am so lonely. He makes a good salary," she added. "And he is good company. Though he could never take Jim's place.

"Of course," she said coyly, "I am not in love. It is just that I am lonely." After Aunt Mag left, Mama scoffed. "In love!" There just may have been a tiny bit of jealousy there. "How ridiculous for a woman her age to talk of being in love. She should be ashamed of herself. She is a marvelous cook, and a good seam-stress. She could make a good living for herself. And not be dependent on a man." She scoffed again. "She claimed to be so very devoted to Jim."

I must have been only about eight years old at the time, but I did not agree with Mama at all about Aunt Mag. "I think it is wonderful Mr. S. wants to marry her, and if he is a nice man, why shouldn't she love him? She is such a lovely woman. She should not be living alone. Then, maybe, she will sing again."

(Aunt Mag did get married to Mr. S., and she did sing again.)

Almost everyone on this street owned their own homes. Only four houses were three stories high (three-deckers). Most of the others were two stories. Our house was a nine-room cottage. It was not a beautiful neighborhood, not impressive, that is, but it was a well-kept-up street. The little handkerchief front lawns were velvety green and well mowed. There were tall shade trees and flowering bushes. The no-nonsense backyards had neat vegetable and flower gardens. To allow your garden to grow thick with weeds was to announce your worthlessness to the neighborhood.

Just a few houses down the street from ours was a small gray house. In this house lived a little boy who was very, very ill. Today, I'm sure it would be called leukemia, but in those days, no one knew just what his ailment was. The doctors knew he was dying, and the little boy knew it too.

I went to visit him often, and read to him the little stories I was fond of writing. And we talked. It was not really sad talk: he laughed a lot at my stories. But he told me of all the things he loved to do, and wondered why he must die. He would look out of his bedroom window and tell me how much he enjoyed the lovely flowers and trees. I thought about him a great deal, and after he died, I wrote a little story about him which I called "The Boy Who Was Afraid of Dying." I still have the clipping, for the old *Boston Post* bought it, and paid me ten dollars for it—a huge sum for a child to earn in those days. I spent a part of it for a few roses to put on his grave.

In those days, when a person in the neighborhood died, there were no formal condolences. There were no funeral homes. The dead person was laid out in the parlor, and a green wreath with a black satin ribbon bow tied on it was hung on the front door, which was kept open. Everyone just walked in, said a prayer, and walked out. The neighbors brought food. The school-children marched in a row from the school to the grave site. There was a short church service, and the relatives gathered for nourishment and to mourn for a few hours, and it was over.

No one in our neighborhood had maids. They had hired girls who sometimes "slept in," but who mostly just came for a few hours a day. We had a hired girl named Emma. We loved Emma. She was like one of the family. In times of stress, she comforted us with hugs and kisses and cookies. She was probably only in her mid-twenties, but she was known as an "old maid." Not too bright (never had much schooling), she was only too happy to work for her board and room. At times when Mama was pregnant, she slept in, did all the cooking and all the laundry, looked after us four children, often acted as midwife if the doctor didn't get there on time, and then cared for the baby. For all of this work she received room and board and, at the end of her stay, five dollars and clothes Mama couldn't wear anymore. This wasn't stinginess on Papa's part. It was the going price. If there was a doctor too, he also received five dollars.

Our parlor had long windows that reached from the ceiling almost to the floor, framed with green velvet draperies. The floor was covered with a flowered Brussels carpet. A beautiful Victorian couch with grape-leaf carving was between the two windows. A lovely mahogany gate-leg table was on another wall. There was a high comb-back rocker, and several other colorful velvet-covered armchairs. And the piano.

Ladies of my mother's sewing circle gathered together in this room, one day a week, and they loved it. I don't recall ever hearing gossip. A little work, a little singing, and, of course, tasty nourishment. As they drank from fragile cups, and nibbled on dainty tidbits, the feathers on their bonnets (which they never removed) trembled and glistened in the sunlight. After the ladies had left, we children were allowed to come in and finish up the refreshments.

Of course Memory Street was not Utopia. A coldness would often arise between two families, especially at election time. And that meant between Democrats and Republicans. There was nothing else. But after the voting was over, the families usually got back on friendly terms.

As there were so many different nationalities in the neighborhood, there were many clubs. It seemed everyone in the neighborhood belonged to a club. Papa, being French, belonged to the Bon-Ami Club. Mama didn't like it too well when Papa spent a complete evening at the Bon-Ami Club. They would have little arguments about it. She always waited up for him, and if he arrived after midnight, there would be some angry words.

At this time, at the age of eight or nine years old, I was doing a little column for the local paper. I called it "Pa Says" or "Ma Says." It was sometimes published, probably more as a joke than anything else, and I received one dollar for it. On one occasion, I wrote down word for word the argument that Mama and Papa had had when he came home late from the Bon-Ami Club. The neighborhood had a good laugh over it, but Mama and Papa were furious with me. That was the end of my column.

Nowadays, boys and girls have their expensive toys, cars they can really ride in, mechanical wonders

to experiment with, expensive bicycles, television sets
of their own in their rooms, and many other things.
But to this day I look back to Memory Street, and I
am grateful for the childhood I had. To this day I am
incapable of making distinctions based on wealth or
position. People are either individuals of good character, or they are not. I can choose my friends. Memory
Street did that for me. And those I loved there still live
on in my heart.

I Remember Grandma

BEFORE GRANDMA AND GRANDPA CAME TO LIVE WITH us for good, they would come to visit us for a long stay, usually in the wintertime. I was delighted to have Grandma come.

For one thing, she took over my chores, which gave me much more time with my beloved books. When Grandma was with us, there were always succulent aromas wafting from the kitchen. She was a marvelous cook. And she taught me how to cook, not from a cookbook, but from her instinct.

Grandpa came from Normandy, but Grandma was the woof and weave of New England. And her remarks were always salty and right to the point. She never measured anything, but did everything "by guess and by golly." A "pinch" of this. A "knife-point" of that. A "smidgen" of this, a few shakes of salt, a "dollop of this, and pour in a little cream," and her dishes always came out just right.

She made wonderful crusty bread and rolls, and when Grandma made bread, we knew there would be fried bread for breakfast. On those mornings there was no need to call me from bed; I'd be at the table early, anticipating that treat. Grandma would take up a piece of the dough she had set to rise on the back of the big black range, a piece about the size of an egg. Then she would flatten it down to about an inch thick, and five or six inches around. Then she would fry it on the griddle with our pure home-churned butter, until it was light brown and crusty on the outside. She would place it on our plates, hot and sizzling. On it we put whatever we liked—maple syrup, golden molasses, or one of Mama's delicious jams or jellies.

My oldest brother was a volunteer member of the Fire Team, and the fire barn was only a few steps from our house. Whenever there was a big fire, Grandma made a huge kettle of "Fireman's Stew" for the tired-out boys. Like Mrs. Murphy's chowder, you could find almost anything edible in Grandma's concoction. A big piece of beef was cut up, browned, and boiled to make the broth, but from then on, she used anything that was on hand. Potatoes, of course, always. Onions, carrots, turnips, parsnips, home-canned tomatoes, any good leftovers in the icebox. And last of all, big, tender dumplings. The firemen came running, and in no time it was gone.

Grandma taught me how to make all the family favorites. Apple pie, for instance. I've never seen apple pie that tasted like Grandma's or that looked like hers. It was high and lumpy, with beautifully crimped edges. For Grandma didn't slice the apples. She just scraped off the peel, and cored them, and cut them in half. These halves she placed, cut side down, in the crust-lined pie plate, very close together. Then she sprinkled them generously with a mixture of spices she created herself, which she called "apple pie spice"—cloves, cinnamon, allspice, ginger, nutmeg, and maybe other spices. Then, a "leetle" flour and a "good measure" of sugar. Then, the top crust. There was no temperature control in the oven. You stuck your hand in, and you knew if it was hot enough. Grandma's pies came out golden brown, and when you cut into them, the sweet, spicy juice spilled out. She never made just one pie, it was usually three or four. And I have seen Grandpa eat half of a big pie for breakfast.

If we children had been good and helpful all day, she would make us a crisp oatmeal confection that tasted like coconut macaroons. I've tried to make it, but it never came out the same as hers did.

Grandma taught me other things too. She impressed on me the fact that it was important to set the table nicely, "to show people that you are somebody." The fork here, the knife there. The table should be ready before the dinner is ready. And "put a flower on the table, even if it is only a wild daisy, and enjoy your pretty china once in a while. To keep it clean, and to make you feel like a queen."

Grandma always had some tricks up her sleeve, too—card tricks and other tricks. One "mind-reading" trick she did was very mysterious to me, until she showed me how to do it. When we had company, she made me her accomplice. She told our guests at dinner that she could, by mental telepathy, let someone know (after sending them out of the room) just which piece of flatware she, or anyone else, had touched. The secret was: *S* (spoon) she would *s*mile, *F* (fork) she would be *f*rowning, *K* (knife) she would be *k*icking a foot up slightly. I would come in, look at her, and announce, "You touched a spoon."

After our noon meal, Grandma would "rense up" and change her voluminous "Mother Hubbard" dress to a black alpaca dress, and over it a snow-white long apron with "Hamburg trim" (a sort of embroidery) or a coarse lace trim. She'd have a little rest, then go to visit a neighbor. She would say, "Your mother don't hold with this, but I'm a friendly person, and I don't like to spread myself too thin." Which only meant that she wasn't about to spend the whole day working.

When the newspaper came in late afternoon, she would turn first to the obituaries. Usually, after a while, she'd put the paper down and sigh, "I don't know a body that's died."

I have regrets about my grandmother. I never gave her the respect or credit due her. I never realized what a lovely lady she was. I recall an incident that impressed this on me. Grandma had scolded me that day, and called me "sassy little girl." And I'm sure I deserved it. But I resented it a little. On the dresser of the room we shared, I saw her gold brooch that she always wore on her black dress. In a spirit of mischief,

I decided to hide it on her. When she missed it, I'm sure she knew I had taken it. "Oh dear!" she said. "Someone must have taken my pin by mistake." Then, in a very gentle voice, "I'm sure it will be back here tonight, as soon as they realize their mistake." Never a scolding word. And you may be sure it *was* back.

Can you hear me, Grandma? I give you your due now. The appreciation and gratitude you deserve. There's a special spot in my heart for you.

Thanksgiving on the Farm

Confused and dismayed by the hurries and haz-ards of now, many a human heart likes, on occasion, to retreat into yesterday. And on Thanksgiving Day I particularly love to recall those times spent on the farm with Grandpa and Grandma, when all the family and relations gathered together.

I try to visualize the old kitchen where so many beautiful meals were prepared. The first thing I see is the big, black range—that was something in its day. It was a wood burner, the base ornamented with scrolls and the big black legs reaching out like giant claws, seeming, to a small child, like a monster ready to crawl and devour.

There were broad warming shelves like engulfing arms that held an interesting assortment—brown calico hot-dish pads, a chipped cup filled with dark tea which Grandma sipped frequently, and, as likely as not, one of Grandpa's corncob pipes. A huge, blue enamel coffeepot simmered on a back lid, and there was always a tin cup of mutton tallow for chaps and chilblains, from which we children suffered, and a homemade cough syrup for which Grandma was famous. And, of course, there was always a soup pot, fragrant and steaming.

The stovepipe was a weird thing, reaching almost to the ceiling, then curving around like a giant cobra until it reached the stained red-brick chimney. Acorn Pride was the stove's name, in nickel letters on the door. And well I should know, because once I got too close to its friendly warmth after a Saturday night bath in the big tin tub, and the words were seared on a little rear cheek for many a day.

I had heard the history of that stove many a time: how, when Grandma was a sixteen-year-old bride and was carried over the threshold for the first time, she ran over to the big range, her husband's wedding gift to her, and embraced it, weeping tears of delight. "Oh! It's beautiful!" she cried. And that very evening there was chicken stew and snowy, flaky biscuits for supper. That was their honeymoon evening.

At Thanksgiving time, the stove was overworked. Grandma started long before the holiday to make the treats she knew we would expect. Pork cake, a fruit-cake using ground salt pork for the shortening, must ripen before serving, so that was made in early September. Snapdoodles (gingersnaps) and Scripture cake (made by rules from the Bible) were also made very early.

Many of these old-time favorites have been forgotten in this day of miracle mixes. But I, a prim little girl of seven or eight, in a starched pinafore, sat at Grandma's table and tasted those delights; and just to think of them still makes my mouth water.

There was a bag pudding, consisting of spiced dough, fruit and nuts. It had to be steamed for hours over a slow fire. Even the bag took longer to make than it would take to open a can of plum pudding today. But the heavenly aroma of that pudding cooking was something you would never forget.

It was warmed over while the dinner was being eaten, and, at serving time, all the family would gather round while it was plopped on a huge platter and topped with a brandy sauce. Then came the big moment when the pudding was set ablaze and carried in by Grandma, while we all sang "Auld Lang Syne."

My favorite treats were big surprises and Kris Kringles. These were cookies—one with a filling of raisins and nuts, the other a spicy, twisted cookie with a lemon icing. But I loved them all. Holy pokes, fruit slumps, snow cake (made with new-fallen snow), whiskey cake (which was forbidden to the little ones, but I always got a taste), and frosty jumbos.

I must have been a very greedy little girl, for I thought of these goodies all day long at school the day before Thanksgiving, while we were having our holiday exercises.

Usually, we left for the farm as soon as school let out. One year, I recall, the snow had been falling softly all morning, and by the time I arrived home it seemed the whole world was covered with a deep, white blanket. The snow was way over my knees, and I was terribly worried that we wouldn't get to the farm.

But Father was getting the sleigh ready, and, inside the house, Mother was busy gathering wraps for us all. Even at the early hour it was almost dark. We children were urged to hurry, to dress warmly and put on boots and scarves. In less than an hour we set off, amid whirling snowflakes and tinkling bells.

At Grandma's, most of the relatives were waiting. There were uncles, aunts, nephews, nieces, other grandmothers and grandfathers, and, for a few years, even some "greats."

Uncle Joe was my favorite . . . with twinkling blue eyes, rosy cheeked, clean-shaven. I can see him now. He would always offer to mash the potatoes. "I'm the world's greatest potato masher," he would say; and as he swung the potato masher he would sing a rather coarse little ditty: "Me and my sweet pertator—and she's a red, little ripe terminator."

Aunt Mary was always asked to say grace. As she blessed the food and the group in a solemn voice, everyone was hushed and still. But the mood didn't last long. A good-natured raucousness and unhampered joking took over as the meal began.

Big bowls of vegetables were carried in, and there was something of just about everything that was grown on Grandpa's farm: Uncle Joe's creamy mashed potatoes, tiny onions in butter, yams, mashed turnips, slivers of carrots with sweet peas, crisp celery on ice water, and all of Grandma's pickles and relishes; no olives, no lettuce, and we never missed them.

And then . . . the grand entrance . . . the huge turkey, its skin crisp and brown to the bursting point and smoking hot, was brought in on the big, blue willow platter. Grandpa did the carving, like a general brandishing his weapons. He stood at the head of the table and spoke to each one of us. "What's for you, Rilla? How about a leg? And you, little Jen, here's your favorite piece, and the wishbone." So it went.

There were always three kinds of stuffing: Grandma's special consisting of bread, ground meat, sage, and seasonings; Father's favorite—chestnut stuffing; and oyster stuffing, which seemed to disappear within minutes. Then there had to be three different kinds of cranberry sauce to please all: whole, jellied, and spiced.

The dining room was warm and fragrant. The walls were red-papered, and there was a potbellied stove. I remember the pictures on the wall: *A Yard of Kittens*, and *Winter Scene* by Currier and Ives. *The Four Seasons of Man*, which had our names handwritten under the pictures, and *Girl with Mitts*, which is still hanging in someone's bedroom. And in the hall, *The Homestead*—which was so like Grandma's house.

Every piece of silver had been polished. Every piece of china glistened. All Grandma's finest pieces were being used. The cut-glass pickle dish, the ruby glass serving dish, the crescent-shaped china dishes for bones at each place. But nothing was ostentatious—just fine and simple. The cloth was white linen darned so meticulously that the repairs could hardly be seen.

Everyone ate until they vowed they could not swallow another bite, then they ate some more. We had to wait for the bag pudding to be served, so we gathered around the old organ to sing while the aunts washed the dishes.

Grandma sang in a thin, sweet voice that made me want to cry—ballads of her time: "Little Brown Jug," and "Rosie O'Grady." Uncle Fred's voice was so deep I was afraid he would choke when he sang, "Down, down, down to the bottom of the sea."

Then, oh! lovely sight, the bag pudding was brought in blazing, and everyone hurried back to the table. Each one was served a slice with brandy hard sauce poured over it. Then came all the other goodies, the pies and the cookies. And the big, blue enamel coffeepot came with them. We couldn't eat all we wanted, but we knew we could take home some of our favorites. My box of goodies was chosen with great care, for I intended it to last a long time.

At last the wonderful, beautiful day was over. For some it would be another year before they would see each other again. For others it was the one and only holiday of the year, the only respite from work. They all left with cries of happiness. "Wonderful time—keep well—see you next year." That was Thanksgiving on the farm. I wish everyone could have such memories.

After the good-byes were over I'm sure Grandma sat in her high-back rocker giving out sighs of contentment, very tired but very happy. She had fought and won the battle of the vittles, and Grandpa, her general, came to give her a loving pat on her shoulder. That was the reward she was waiting for, the only reward she wanted.

Thanksgiving is still a big day in New England, and still a day of feasting. But oh! how different it is. The relatives may walk in a half-hour ahead of time (if they come at all). No help is needed in the kitchen, and there probably would be no room for them anyway. Everything comes ready for the oven. The turkey, already dressed, is taken from the freezer, and the stuffing is made from a package in a few moments. The pickles come from the store, the cranberry sauce from a can, and the vegetables from a cellophane bag dropped into boiling water for a few minutes.

The can of plum pudding is opened with an electric opener, and warmed a little. The mincemeat is taken from a jar and put into a crust that came between two cardboard disks (frozen). And the whipped cream is squirted from a tall can. And nobody eats too much: "I'm on a diet. . . . This ulcer, you know. . . . Do you have any Maalox?"

And long before dark the last guest has gone. "Must be going before the heavy traffic." But for me, and mine, it's still a great day.

Recipes from Thanksgiving on the Farm

Here are some of the recipes from those memorable Thanksgivings.

KRIS KRINGLES

4 cups flour (filled lightly)
Pinch of salt
½ teaspoon cinnamon
½ teaspoon ginger
¼ teaspoon nutmeg
½ cup solid shortening
½ cup sugar
1 whole egg
1 scant cup dark molasses
a dash of vinegar
1 teaspoon baking soda
½ cup boiling water
¼ cup chopped nutmeats
½ cup chopped raisins

Sift the flour with the salt and spices. Cream the shortening and sugar together. Add the egg. Beat together with the flour mixture. Add the molasses and vinegar. Dissolve the soda in the boiling water, and add to the other ingredients. The dough should be thick enough to drop without threading. Add the nuts and raisins.

Drop by double teaspoonfuls on greased cookie sheets: first one teaspoonful, then overlapping that with another. Mark the center with a fork to give a twisted look. Be sure to leave room for the dough to spread. Bake 8 to 10 minutes at 350°F.

This recipe will make about 25 large cookies. They taste better if kept a while in a crock. Ice with thin lemon icing (recipe below).

LEMON ICING

1 cup confectioners' sugar
2 tablespoons butter (softened)
1 teaspoon lemon extract
1 tablespoon boiling water

Mix all the ingredients and beat until creamy. Use a few drops more water if needed. Spread thinly on cookies.

SNOW CAKE

¼ cup white shortening
1 cup white sugar
1½ cups sifted flour
1 teaspoon vanilla extract
1 teaspoon baking powder
Pinch of salt
1 tablespoon whole milk
1 cup new-fallen snow
4 egg whites (save yolks for custard)
Granulated sugar

Cream the shortening with half the sugar, until it is very light and creamy. Sift in the flour very slowly. Add the vanilla, baking powder, and salt, then beat in the milk alternately with the clean, new-fallen snow, a little of each at a time (never use old snow). Beat the egg whites until very stiff. Now, add the remaining sugar alternately with the egg whites.

Bake in a greased deep round pan for about 45 minutes in a 350°F oven. Frost with snow icing (recipe below), then sprinkle on a little granulated sugar for a frosty effect.

Grandma served this cake with cup custards—a delicious treat!

SNOW ICING

1 cup confectioners' sugar
1 tablespoon soft butter or margarine
1 tablespoon new-fallen snow
1 tablespoon light cream
1 stiffly beaten egg white
1 teaspoon vanilla extract

Cream the sugar and the butter or margarine. Add the snow and cream. Add the egg white and beat until very creamy.

What Kids Did for Fun
in the Early 1900s

Very few of the things we kids used to do for fun are known to the present generation. Television, radio, computers, and high-tech toys have taken over. How many little boys today own a bag of marbles? Have they ever heard of agates, shinies, and pooners? In those days, marbles were a boy's treasures. And what little girls own a bag of jackstones? Do they know about onesies, twosies, and threesies? I carried my little bag of jackstones and my little rubber ball everywhere.

Mumbletypeg, a jackknife game, was very popular with the boys, and every boy carried a jackknife, either in his pocket or in his boot top. Horse-chestnut battles (played with a nut on a string) were a dangerous game, but, in season, it was very popular. Wrestling was a big thing for the boys, usually in the schoolyard at recess—resulting in many bloody noses.

For some games boys and girls joined together. One of them was hopscotch. If there was a tar or cement sidewalk in front of a house it was always marked up with oblongs and squares for hopscotch. It was played with a small stone thrown into a square, and you hopped on one foot until you reached it without stumbling, and without hopping on any of the chalk lines. If you stumbled you were out. Mother complained that shoes wore out so quickly. That was because of hopscotch.

Fun wasn't planned in those days; it just happened. If a group of boys and girls got together, eventually someone would suggest something. For example, "Let's jump off steps." Do boys and girls today ever jump off steps? We would invade any porch that had a flight of steps. We would start on the lowest one, and keep going higher. If we could jump from the highest one, we would then look for a higher flight.

Once in a while you'd go one step too high, and get the wind knocked out of you, or sprain your ankle or worse. Very often someone would come to the door and yell, "What are you trying to do—break your neck?" I don't recall anyone ever breaking a neck, but breaking a leg was not unknown.

One boy, Danny, who lived across the street, did just that. He was our champion jumper. He had mastered the top step of the highest flight of steps we knew of. Then he decided that jumping from the porch railing (higher than the top step) would mark his finest hour. So he perched there. We all yelled,

"Don't do it, you'll break your neck!" We warned him, "Your mom will kill you if she finds out." But he flexed his knees and jumped—and broke his leg. But his mom didn't kill him. She visited him every day in the hospital, took him sweets and toys. Everyone made a fuss over him. And we all had the thought, "Gosh! I wish I'd break a leg. No school, and all that attention." But afterwards, Danny always walked with a slight limp.

We had roller skates in those days. Not the fancy ones like today, white leather shoes with pompoms on them, but metal skates that rusted in no time, and which you strapped on your own shoes, with thin leather straps and buckles that never stayed put for long. We had ice skates too, and they were not much better.

I had weak ankles and could never skate well, but my sister—she was the skater. I envied her. She'd have such a great time. While I would be falling every minute, she would be flying around the pond, her braids swinging out in the wind, often hand in hand with some boy, arms crossed in front of them. I would go around the pond once, ending up with wet, torn pants, skinned knees and knuckles, and one mitten lost, and usually crying. My hair never blew in the wind, my cheeks never got pink, I just looked miserable, and I was. I soon gave up.

In the early summer evenings, after supper, the girls and boys of our neighborhood usually joined together for games. We'd play "Relievo," a hide-and-seek game, "Run, Sheep, Run," a tag game, or "Run, Thief, Run," a running game. And always popular was jump rope. We had our champion jumpers too. We'd jump rope to verses: "My old man is a funny old man, washes his face in a frying pan. Combs his hair with the leg of a chair, my old man is a funny old man."

We had hundreds of verses to sing with the rope jumping, some of them senseless. "Inti minti tippity fig, dina dona norma nig. Oats, floats, creaky notes, dina dona norma nig." Every child had a jump rope, and some of them were quite fancy, with pearl or ivory handles and bright-colored rope.

Often, in the summer evenings, when it was too warm to run, we played games sitting on the front steps. These were guessing games, charades, question and answer games; or we would ask riddles—conundrums, they were called—which were very popular. Or we would just talk children's gossip. Our front steps were a favorite gathering place, as there were four of us under eleven. We sat out there until Papa would come to the door and say "Scat. It's time for bed."

One of the most daring things for kids to do for fun was to open the door of Oscar's car. And run. Oscar was a grown man, mentally ill but harmless. There were not many cars around at that time (1904), not in our neighborhood at least. But Oscar had an old abandoned and useless car which he kept at the end of a lane, with everything he owned in it. He didn't sleep in it, unless it was raining, but slept in a grove right near it, on a blanket.

He must have had a little money, as he seemed to have food. He ate his meals on a little stool he set up by the side of his car. He never bothered anyone, and the authorities never bothered him. Perhaps the town gave him a little money. He didn't work, but was often seen with a bag and pick, picking up trash along the street and in the park.

If we played a game that required a forfeit, that was usually the forfeit one had to pay. To open the door of Oscar's car and run. I did it once, and saw that everything in the car was arranged neat and clean, and it even smelled good. And on the backseat were a few wildflowers in a vase. I'm ashamed now that we did such a thing. I don't know if Oscar could talk. I never heard him speak, but then, I never got very close to him. He was very ugly. The boys taunted him, too: "Oscar, Oscar, Oscar Rugg, Crazy as a big bedbug." But he never seemed to resent it. Perhaps he didn't hear either.

Another dare was to open the door of a synagogue and look in. The synagogue was in a storefront on a nearby street. There were lots of Catholic kids in our neighborhood, and for them it was a real dare, as their priest had forbidden them to do so. I did it once, and I was very surprised to see that it was so nice in there. Cool, and spotless, and pretty, with red cushions on the chairs, in neat rows and circles. And someone was seated at the small organ, playing and singing a sad, sweet song. I felt like lingering. But I didn't dare.

I was really chicken at heart. I never had the courage to walk into Johnnie's Soda Shop, the favorite hangout of the Forty Johns and Mollies, a local gang of teenagers who had a very bad reputation. They often invaded the recreation places, and made trouble. So you see, we had those problems then, also. But for us kids—life was simple, and life was fun. We didn't need TV and VCRs. We made our own happy times.

Papa's Garden

WHEN ONE IS GETTING OLD, ANYTHING THAT HAS SOME link with old times, any memory that brings back happy days of youth, has rare value; it can change a mood from depression to smiling reminiscence very quickly. Papa's garden is something I like to think about. I was about ten years old at the time, and it was a big thing in my life.

Today, patios with sputtering barbecue grills and wrought-iron or redwood furniture, colorful hanging lanterns at night, and a general air of relaxation have taken over backyard gardens . . . and that's nice and very good for the family. But, not so many years ago, little "truck" gardens were the principal decor for backyards, thriving little gardens filled with the most popular vegetables: tomatoes, radishes, cucumbers, onions, beets, cabbages, and, sometimes, even a patch of corn.

Almost every home in our neighborhood had a garden. In fact, they were just as much a character symbol and a status indicator as today's pleasure car. A family that had no garden was either shiftless or lazy or both—or they had to be wealthy, and there were no wealthy people in our neighborhood. To have a garden and not take care of it was a disgrace. Having a garden full of weeds was like waving your worthlessness in your neighbor's face.

Papa was not a gardener by instinct, so he substituted perseverance for a green thumb. If his seeds didn't come up in what he thought was the required time, he planted again and again. Then, often we had to pull out half the seedlings. But his joy at seeing green onion tips and tiny beet tops peeping through the sod was something to see. "Look," he would say in his beautiful French (for he always spoke French when he was excited), "look, again a miracle."

In late winter, the catalogs came. Papa studied them industriously. The pictures were glorious, the promises supreme. True, the finished product was never quite as beautiful, but if it grew, and it was delicious in spite of bumps and blemishes, he was content. First came the planning on paper. Usually, on a cold and stormy winter night, Papa would map out his garden: radishes here, beets there, all with a great deal of argument from Mama and us children.

"I want that corner for my gourds," Mama would protest.

"I want a big spot for flower seeds," my voice chimed in. "Mama promised." I always entered my flowers in the county fair.

"I want a space for my Halloween pumpkins." That was my brother.

And my little sister pleaded, "Don't forget I want some 'tunias." She would rather plant flowers than eat, and she would eat cereal only if the package contained a packet of flower seeds.

The very first warm evening we all went out to drive stakes in the still-hard earth, measuring and marking out our sections. Cords were stretched between the stakes so that the rows would be straight and even. Many a time, another snowstorm came and covered our stakes before we could plant a thing.

On the first day of May, unless it was snowing, Papa was up bright and early, and got my grumbling brother out of bed to help him with the digging. The ground was still hard and cold, but that was the day to dig. Mama had a theory that the seeds should be sown with the full of the moon. "They'll never sprout otherwise," she declared solemnly. "You'd just be wastin'." But Papa couldn't wait for the moon. He could already taste those sweet little peas and succulent tomatoes.

By the middle of May, if luck was with us weatherwise, the tiny shoots were showing. Then, after school, we were urged, sometimes not too gently, to get out the rakes and the hoes. No time now for marbles and jackstones and hopscotch; our reputation was at stake. It was our pride that was being challenged. "This year," Papa would say, "we are going to show 'em."

Papa worked with us and we liked to work with Papa; so, at first we didn't mind. It was fun to be outdoors after supper, after being indoors all winter, and the air was cool and sweet. But, long before the seeds matured, it became hot, and we became frustrated with the everlasting and ever-growing weeds. And Papa had sort of lost his enthusiasm and was leaving more and more to us. We became rebellious, and it was only Mama's promise of the wonderful meals to come that kept us at our tasks — that and our pride.

Then came the worms . . . and the bugs. They were supposed to be snatched from the plants and put into tin cans, then destroyed; how I hated this work. It was not girl's work, I protested. Gooey, slimy things! The potato bugs I hated worst of all — horrid, smelly, and hard. Sometimes one of my brothers would chase me with one in his fingers, trying to put it down my back. I hollered. I screamed. And, to this day, I don't care much for potatoes.

But the boys had to do the cultivating; and when we heard them complaining about their aching backs and blistered hands, we smiled with a revenging smile. Things were growing so fast now, and it was real work for them; they couldn't let up, even for a day. Papa had suddenly become busy with other things. The grape arbor had to be trimmed, the fence had to be mended, his tools all needed sharpening, and so on. He went out to look at the garden every day. And he might pick off a leaf or a bug, but that was the extent of his labor.

There came a morning when we rushed back into the house. "Ma! Ma! There's a red tomato. Come see it. Ma! A red tomato." Up to that time, we'd had only the peas and a few little radishes. The peas were certainly delicious, but they were gone in a few days. Now, the promise was being fulfilled, and Mama showed her pleasure with a childish exclamation: "Oh! I'd give my hat for a salad of ripe tomato slices on a bed of fresh garden lettuce."

Papa wouldn't let anyone touch it. The next day he plucked the tomato, sliced it, and carried it on a plate to Mama, just as she sat down to eat. He took all the credit. "For you, Your Majesty, the first fruit of my garden." But Mama got up and reached up to the top shelf for the silver cruet stand that had belonged to my grandmother, filled the bottles with oil and vinegar, sprinkled some on the tomato, and shared it with us children. Now, we were ready for the garden.

In the meantime, we were enjoying the last of the garden peas. We girls shelled the precious things carefully while sitting out on the porch in the sun. The trees were in bud, the birds were singing. Soon we'd be eating the tender globes, pungent and sweet, in a buttery broth with thick slices of crusty homemade bread . . . a simple supper, but food fit for the gods.

Every once in a while, I'd pop one of the green pods in my mouth, savoring its juices, chewing it slowly to make it last. A few of the larger pods I would save for my little brothers to sail in a tub. We'd make little paper sails for them, and tiny paper dolls for passengers. Children were easily amused in those days. They don't seem to like things like that anymore.

The first potatoes that came were very small, but those were the ones I loved, and the only ones I would eat. Mama scrubbed them, but did not peel them. She steamed them in a very little water and some fresh butter. We ate them just like that—taking them up in our fingers and biting into them. When the larger ones came, she'd cut them in quarters and cook them quickly. She would then drain them, pour a cream sauce over them with some lumps of butter, and put a few thin slices of cheese on top before browning them in the oven for a few minutes.

Potato digging was a task for the whole family, and sometimes a few of the neighbor's boys too. Mama would bring out a jug of cold drink. We called it vinegar water, but farmers call it "slunk" (cold water, vinegar, ginger, and sugar). It tasted better than any cola of today. Big mugs of this with a plate of her sugar cookies were enough of a bribe to make any boy glad to come over and help. We sat under the gnarled old apple trees to eat and drink. And why we laughed so heartily, I can't remember.

When we had snap beans in the garden, both yellow and green, I loved to pick them and eat them raw. I had no sooner filled a big pan than they were on the big black range bubbling merrily, along with a big wedge of bacon rind, or a ham bone with lots of meat on it. The fragrance spilled over into the summer air, and we knew we would have a succulent and satisfying supper that night. The beans were thick and meaty. Sometimes Mama cooked herb dumplings with them . . . so good! I try, but I can't seem to make them taste as they used to.

And there were so many things we'd eat raw. We never went hungry between meals. A tender carrot pulled from the ground, put under cold water a moment, took the place of a sweet. And a tiny cucumber with a sprinkling of salt tasted so good with a crisp cracker, or a little raw onion with a thick slice of buttered bread, even a raw potato if we were real hungry—crisp, crunchy food for the soul.

One day brother Will went out to pick a cucumber. He came running back into the house. "A snake!" he shouted. "A big snake in the garden. It's a killer! Come quick, Pa!" We all ran out.

It was a snake, and it was a big one. Such large snakes were rare in this part of the country. It was about half an inch thick, and about a yard long. Papa yelled, "Stand back, children." I thought he looked pale and trembly. "We'd better get the fire department."

Mama looked at him rather scornfully. She quickly broke off a big branch from the old cherry tree, poked it under the snake, picked it up and threw it in the trash can. Then she threw a match into the trash can. That was the end of the snake. Papa had nothing to say. But I was old enough to have thought, "This time, it was the snake that was expelled from the garden, and Eve was triumphant."

Early fall was a busy time for us all. Mama would make many things from Papa's garden. Catsup, chili sauce, piccalilli, relishes of corn and green tomato, mincemeat, pickles (sweet and sour, and dill). What a treasure to store these things in our big cabinet in the cellar, for the cold winter to come. We loved to see the jars lined up day by day, rubbing our tummies at the thought of the good eating to come.

Now, Papa was in his glory. He would tighten all the jars that Mama had processed during the day. Then we'd help him to carry them to the cellar, singing as we went, all his favorite songs: "Sweet Rosie O'Grady," "Roamin' in the Gloamin'," "Rivière de Loup," "Little Brown Jug," and others.

We were so proud of the shining rows of jellies and jams shining on the window sills, a rainbow of colors—reds, purples and greens, and shades in between. We had a share in these, too, for we had helped to pick the grapes from the vines and the plums and cherries and pears from the trees.

We were fortunate children and, as I look back, I'm glad we were there then. I would have hated to miss Papa's garden.

Welcome, Peddlers

ONE OF THE THINGS THAT BRIGHTENED OUR LIVES WHEN I was a child was the familiar figure of the pack peddler.

Nowadays, the few remaining door-to-door salesmen are sometimes suspect as high-pressure salesmen, and often considered a nuisance; back then, no one was hostile to the peddler. We welcomed him. He was a part of everyday life in the early 1900s. Very often, if he had come a long way, he was given food and drink and even a night's lodging. In return he would leave gifts for the family: a few spools of thread, a small piece of yard goods, tiny trinkets for the children.

Actually the farmer's wife had little in the way of entertainment, and a visit from the peddler was a big thing in her life, almost a social occasion. Sometimes it was the only break in a long day of household chores. He brought the news of the day also. He knew the trend of the times, what was going up, what was going down. We asked his advice.

I can remember my grandmother dressed for the afternoon in her black alpaca gown, with a white apron with wide bands of lace, anxiously scanning the street, waiting for the peddler we knew only as "Pete." She had been looking for him for two or three days. Pete came by as regularly as clockwork early in the first week of each month, just before suppertime. He took his heavy pack from his back, and out would come a wondrous array of merchandise.

Oh! To be able to buy all those things. There were lacy handkerchiefs, colorful scarfs, socks and stockings, combs and brushes, small rugs, brooches, jewelry, even wedding rings. Mother and Grandma frugally picked the things they needed. Then, if there was any money left, we children could each buy a small item—a tiny jointed doll, a spinning top, a bottle of rose water. These things seldom cost more than a penny.

But even if we had no money to buy, Pete always had a tiny gift for each of us, after the transaction was completed. For years I kept a small tin trunk, stenciled in color, which Pete had given me. His earnings must have been pitifully small, yet he could always afford to give us a bit of his stock.

There was another peddler who came to us often. This was the Oriental rug man. His roll, which he carried on his back, was so heavy and bulky that I never could figure out how he could carry it. He was such a little man. One day he showed us the heavy straps that went around his shoulders, back and front, to even out the burden. His back was very bent, no doubt from all those years of bending under that heavy load.

Many of the rugs on our floor we had bought from him. They were good rugs that wore for years and years. And cheap—though at that time, we thought that to pay ten dollars for a rug was extravagant indeed. Later on, dishonest rug dealers appeared, and their rugs were shoddy imitations of the true Oriental rugs. They fell apart after a few cleanings.

The earliest peddlers, way back in the late 1800s and early 1900s, came from foreign countries, and had to learn to speak English. They worked very hard, and they were respected. Many of today's biggest merchants carry names that once belonged to these peddlers, men who sold from packs on their backs until they became prosperous enough to buy a horse and wagon.

For immigrants it was the quickest way to get started on the road to fortune in America. And certainly one of the quickest ways to learn the language.

The Oriental rug man was a very sweet man, gentle and soft-spoken. He always gave my oldest sister (then about twelve years old) the nicest trinket. He told my mother that he would like to marry her one day, when he had accumulated more money. We all thought this was a big joke. I thought of him as an old man. And my sister was young and beautiful. I found out later that he was only twenty-eight years old at that time, and he did become wealthy. A newcomer could start earning the day he left the boat, investing in a few pairs of shoelaces, making a few cents profit, then buying more. In a few weeks he had enough money to invest in pens, pencils, matches, and other small items, selling them and repeating, and making a small profit each time. When he finally bought a horse and wagon, it was his home, as well as his transportation.

There are many places in New England, and all over the country, that became industrial cities because they served as peddlers' headquarters. These industries developed as the peddlers prospered and began manufacturing their own products.

Then there was another kind of peddler — the "medicine man." At first he peddled licorice, bitter aloes, homemade ointments, sassafras, herbs, and flavorings. Later, he went into business in a big way, with his "medicine show." He gathered a few Indians to trail along with their families, and usually an old Indian chief. The old Indian chief was supposed to be the creator of the remedy the medicine man was selling. It would cure anything, he claimed, from an aching tooth to tuberculosis.

One of these was the "Kickapoo" medicine show. I clearly recall attending this show with my family. It was held in a nearby field. The Indians did a war dance in full regalia, though rather shabby, then they smoked a peace pipe and chanted. That was the show.

Then the medicine man went into his spiel. "Only fifty cents a bottle, friends, for this wonderful medicine that will make you feel young again." Fifty cents was a lot of money then, half a day's wages, but the hands went up. "Here! Here! Here!" In less than an hour he had sold all his stock. They spent the next day brewing more.

Someone once said that for immigrants, peddling was the preparatory school of America. And looking back over the years, I can well believe that it was so.

Ma Bell Had Nothing over
"Hello, Central"

I'M QUITE SURE WE HAD THE FIRST TELEPHONE IN OUR neighborhood in West Boylston. It must have been 1904. I was about ten years old.

I have read that the first words ever said over the telephone (by Alexander Graham Bell in 1876) were, "Mr. Watson, come here, I want you," and that he wished to have the standard response be, "Hoy-Hoy-Hoy."

But that wasn't the way it turned out. And I remember well the thrill, when each of us was urged to crank the handle and say, "Hello, Central." And Central (whose name in our area was Sarah) answered gaily, "Hello, welcome newcomers."

Our lives changed from that day. God was undoubtedly the center of the universe, but Central was undoubtedly the center of *our* existence. There was never a dull moment. We called Central for anything and everything.

It was a six-party line, and each party had a different ring. Ours was one long and one short. But we answered all of them, and it kept us busy. We knew everyone's business, and everyone knew ours.

Central was called upon to dispense a vast store of knowledge. She was an animated dictionary, a nurse, a living news sheet, and a troubleshooter. She called everyone by their first names. If you didn't know someone's number, you just asked her to get "Mary." And she would. Or she might answer, "Mary isn't home. I just saw her walking down the street." Or, "Mary isn't feeling well today, you had better go see her."

Between intervals of getting numbers, she would be kept busy answering questions: "I smell smoke. Is there a fire anywhere?" "Central, the church bell is tolling—who died?" "Central, my clock stopped. What time is it?" "Central, is old lady Williams any better today?" "Central, how long must I cook apple jelly?" "Central, will you spread it around that I have a braided rug for sale?"

Those were just routine, ordinary, everyday questions. But, if an election was going on, Central would keep everyone posted as to the results. If there was a bad storm, she was supposed to know what damage had been done. If the "Black Maria" (ambulance) went by, the lines would be buzzing, everyone curious to know who it was. Not only would she answer these questions with accuracy, but she would obligingly give out the latest bulletins on their condition.

"I'll just call Central," Mama would say, "and find out if Mr. King is any better this morning. No need to bother the family, Central will know." And, if the worst happened, Central was a clearinghouse for all the details pertinent to the funeral arrangements: the pallbearers, calling the minister, and ordering the flowers.

She was an authority on train schedules, and often offered to call the out-of-town relatives. She had close ties with other small-town operators, and they worked together. "I think I'll call Central," Mama would say, "and see if she can talk to Mary's brother John in Webster, to tell him that Mary is poorly." I think Central would have been really hurt if we had asked for our party by number. She would have thought we didn't trust her.

A long-distance call was a rare event in those long-ago days, and anyone who made one was slightly nervous about it. But you didn't need to memorize a string of numerals. You just left it to Central. "Central, I want to talk to my brother in Hartford. His name is John King." She didn't ask you his number, or his street address. But she would ask if there was anything wrong. Was someone ill? And, in no time at all, John was on the phone.

Women at home, caught in some emergency, would call Central to locate a husband or straying child. "Central, this is Susan. Have you seen Frank around? I need him. Paulie has hurt himself." Or, "Hello, Central, if you see my Ellen around, tell her to go to the store and buy some sugar. I want to make some cookies." And chances were that Ellen would soon be home with the wanted sugar.

Mama was pretty lenient about eavesdropping. Everyone did it. It was a common pastime in a dull age. I don't believe anyone seriously objected. And everyone became very careful to learn cryptic little half-statements, meaningful only to those in the know. Central herself used many little tricks, half-truths, and evasive answers if she didn't want others to understand.

After our phone was installed, we never felt alone. Central was always there. It was a great comfort to know that we always could call on her. Roads might be blocked with snow, bridges might be washed out, great trees thrown across the road in a bad storm and a great wind. Central couldn't prevent these disasters, of course, but she kept us informed, and upon occasion gave us help.

There were times when a woman was in labor, and the doctor could not be located. Central usually knew where the doctor was. It would never occur to the doctor to go out on a call without alerting her first. And in an emergency, she followed up quickly. We all used that relaying service, and it was a godsend.

She could be the guardian of happy occasions as well. A golden anniversary would often be announced by her, and a celebration followed. Birthdays, graduations, and promotions were all good news she loved to spread around.

Nowadays, the whole responsibility of getting a long-distance call rests on my shoulders (direct dialing). If, in my excitement, I place a finger on the wrong digit, I get an impersonal recording telling me I have committed a boo-boo, and I'd best hang up and try again. And no one gives a hoot. Central wasn't like that. If you gave a wrong number, she knew right away, and corrected you gently. And there was your party.

By the time I was fourteen, things had changed. Almost all the neighbors had phones. They had spread like wildfire. At that time there were more than ten thousand subscribers. The company had built a smart new headquarters on Norwich Street, with a large central office force. The thin little pamphlet of numbers had changed to a thick little book.

By then, between the electric company and the telephone company, Worcester streets were a maze of wires and cables. By 1930, the telephone company had moved its headquarters from Norwich Street to a much larger and more imposing building on Elm Street, to accommodate the many new customers and to do justice to the many new services.

Today's modern telephone services are miracles of technology and convenience. I can dial anyone I wish to talk to in the United States, or Canada, or Uganda, bouncing a message off a satellite with a flick of a finger, or a push of a tiny button. And (who knows?) perhaps in the future, someone will be able to communicate with Venus, or the moon.

But, for me, there will always be a soft spot in my heart for our Sarah, who was "Hello, Central." She was the heart and soul of the community. Man has not yet invented a gadget that will replace a heart. And I doubt that he ever will.

Those Old-Time Bees

IN THE LATE 1800S AND THE VERY EARLY 1900S, "BEES" of all kinds were the important social functions of the year. There were spelling bees and husking bees, quilting bees and barn-raising bees. And there may have been other kinds of bees I have forgotten about.

When I was about eight years old, and took part in my first spelling bee, I came in third. I failed on the word *gnome*, which was a rather difficult word for an eight-year-old child. A nine-year-old girl spelled it correctly.

All the neighbors who could walk came to the spelling bee. There was standing room only after 7 P.M. A delicious buffet of homemade pastries was served afterwards, and the winner honored. It was an integral part of the school system. Occasionally, there were spelling bees for adults also, the fathers, mothers, sisters, and brothers of the pupils, and these were very exciting events that no one wanted to miss. Days of preparation would go into them, for it was a rare chance to shine in public. The winner was a hero or heroine for months afterwards.

The contest might last for many hours, the words growing harder and harder and the excitement rising to fever pitch, as one after another of the contestants failed. And "officers of the law" stood, one on each side of the room, to keep the audience quiet (or try to).

"Silence," they kept shouting, as the audience attempted to help the contestant with mouth signs or finger signs. But the murmurs became louder and louder each time the teacher declared the contestant "Wrong! Sit down!" Finally only two remained standing, a boy and a girl.

"Spell *reparable*." This happened at the last spelling bee I attended in 1904. It was not such a difficult word, but the boy spelled it with an *e* where there should have been an *a*. The excitement was intense as the teacher shouted "Wrong!" For the boy realized his mistake as soon as he had spelled it, and was trying to correct it. "Wrong! Wrong!" shouted the teacher. "Sit down! Sit down!" He slumped in his chair, and the girl spelled it correctly. Hers was the triumph and the glory. She was the heroine of the evening. The prize? A box of chocolates perhaps, or a bouquet of flowers. What matter? She was a star!

The husking bees were the favorite of the young people. Corn was husked to put in the silo, and for each red ear that a boy found, he was entitled to a kiss from a favorite among the girls. Then the barn was cleared for the feasting and the dancing.

Barn-raising bees were not only very popular, but

very necessary. No farmer would think of hiring a builder to build him a barn. If wind or fire or lightning destroyed a barn, the neighbors would have a bee to rebuild it. After all, what were neighbors for? The men would gather on weekends, early in the day, and by the end of the first day the framework would be up. The women gathered to cook up a storm, and gossip while they cooked. Then everyone would sit together at the long table, or several tables put together, to enjoy the hearty meal—roast pork, baked potatoes, all kinds of vegetables, pies, cakes and puddings, plenty of hot coffee. Tired as they were, they felt good after such a meal. Then someone would start to play the fiddle or the accordion, and no one was too tired to dance, and drink cider and homemade root beer and ginger beer. Young people would stroll arm in arm in the meadow.

Quilting bees were very popular when I was a child, but after 1900 they went out of style. Quilting is back now, but it is done from kits, with the design already planned, and all the materials to work with in a package. It is now a single-person project. But in the old days, a quilting bee was a very festive occasion. The women would arrive early in the morning. They would work diligently and deftly all morning, their tongues going as fast as their fingers. They would discuss the sick, the newly married, the dead, and the absent, who was "keepin' company," who wasn't getting along. (There was no such thing as divorce.) By noon they had the quilts ready to put on the frames, and they were hungry. They had all brought box lunches with their names on them. Now, the young people joined them. The girls had their lunchboxes with names written on them in very large script. The boys came, supposedly to bring the frames from the attic and set them up. But mostly, it was to entice the girls to come. The girls' lunchboxes were gathered for the boys to bid on. If a box brought a dollar (the highest bid), you knew that girl was either very popular, or was known for the good things in her box. Then, of course, the bidder ate with the girl whose box he had bought. There was plenty for two. Very often the event ended up in an engagement.

Then the frames were set up, and work would begin again, with everyone pitching in. The money collected was used to buy materials needed. These quilts were very beautiful, very colorful, and very clever in design. All the fairs and expositions of the day had quilt shows. (It varied in different states, but usually, if a covering was simply lined it was called a quilt. But if it was padded and lined and tied with many tiny bows, either narrow satin ribbon or yarn, it was called a comforter, or sometimes a "quilt-comforter.")There were historic quilts, biblical quilts, and memory quilts. The memory quilts were made from hundreds of pieces of famous clothing of the families — wedding dresses, children's party dresses, bonnets, satin coats, and the like.

I recall that Aunt Martha made such a memory quilt once. She worked on it for years. Every stitch was done by hand, very tiny, so you could barely see them. All the pieces were diamond-shaped. She called the pattern "Diamond Whirl." Pieces of her own wedding dress were in it, mostly silks and satins and velvets. It was a very beautiful thing, and won many prizes. I was so impressed with this quilt of Aunt Martha's, I wrote a poem about it, many years ago. And here it is.

THE COMFORTER

"I made this quilt," the woman said
As she rose a little from her bed.
In the forgotten room, her shape a blur,
Flickering shadows surrounded her.
"I made it from things they used to wear."
Rainbow remnants, stitched with care.
Pieces of warmth, where past thoughts meet,
Gathered with love, and fitted so neat.
They call it a "quilt," but it's a comforter to me,
I place my hand, here and there, and all of them
*   I see.*
And her pallor changed to palest rose,
As she lay back in sweet repose.
"They never leave you, your loved ones, you know,
You can keep them with you. I'm telling you so!"
I had brought food for comforting,
And good thoughts to share with tea;
But I left unsure of my success
For SHE had comforted ME!

When Mama's Ship Comes In

I NEVER HEARD OF MOTHER'S DAY WHEN I WAS A SMALL child. We were a big family and our mother was the most important person in our lives. We always treated her that way.

She was a wonderful manager, but there was not always ready money to buy what we needed immediately. At such times I would be puzzled to hear her say, "Just wait until my ship comes in! Then you'll have everything you want."

We lived in Worcester, and I had never seen the ocean. So I had never seen any big ships. The only ships I had ever seen were passenger boats on Lake Quinsigamond.

I had seen pictures, though, of large ships with great white sails. I knew such a ship could never come into our lake, and I began to worry about it. I knew it would be a great day for Mama when her ship came in, but when and where?

"Where is your ship going to land, Mama?" I would ask. And she would answer, "Don't you fret, when my ship comes in, I will know where it is going to land."

"What's it going to have in it?" I would keep teasing. "It will be loaded with money and all sorts of good things," she'd answer, laughing merrily. Then she'd give me a little push. "Go out and play now, Jennie, don't bother me anymore."

Mama was very fond of tossing proverbs, quotes, and maxims at us, many of which I'm sure she made up herself. If my sister and I quarreled and fought, she would say, "Pretty is as pretty does, and right now, you are both ugly." When she caught us putting on lipstick (we were about eight and ten years old), she said, "A smile on your lips is better than tricks."

She had sayings galore about the weather. "Red sky in the morning, sailor take warning." "Blue sky enough to cover a dime—rain will stop and sun will shine." "Rain before seven, clear before eleven." "Rainbow in the sky, good time nearby." "Tears won't make the sun shine, but smiles might."

When Mama's winter skirts became faded or worn, she cut up the good parts for mittens. One evening when she was sewing them, I asked her why we couldn't have bought mittens.

"A penny saved is a penny earned," she said. "If I can get ten pairs of mittens out of this old skirt, that could save me five dollars. Five dollars could buy you each a new dress and maybe something else besides. Every penny counts."

"Make over—make do, make good as new. Wear 'til it's done, then to the bank run."

At one time, Mama kept a few chickens, one of which was a hen that kept trying to crow. "A whistling woman, and a crowing hen, will always come to some bad end," quoted Mama. She thought it was bad luck to have a hen crowing all the time. "We'll have to get rid of that one." So she proceeded to prepare the hen for the pot, and we had chicken and dumplings. But I could not understand why the hen was not still "bad luck," so I refused to eat it.

If Mama's nose itched, she insisted company was coming. If she dropped a knife, that was a sign a man was coming. And if she dropped a fork, then it was a woman on the way.

Every time Mama sneezed, there was always a big, loud "God bless" to keep her from getting a cold. But if any of us sneezed, she'd run for the sulfur and molasses. Two or three sneezes would mean castor oil.

There was one time I needed, or wanted, a new dress very badly. "Mama," I said, "I sure wish your ship would come in." She became irritated with me then, and told me to go out and play. "It will come in when it's time, and not before," she said.

But I worried about it. I must have been about ten years old at the time, surely old enough to know better. But I'd lie awake at night and wonder who would let her know when it did come in, and how awful it would be if she missed it.

Sometimes, on bad days, when we'd have to be in the house all day, we would get very noisy and quarrelsome. Mama would get very impatient with us. And she would say, "I just wish I could go stay on an island for a while — so far away that you couldn't even send me a penny postcard. I'd love it. I'd read and take long walks, all by myself. It would be heaven."

We stopped quarreling then, very shocked that Mama would even think of leaving us. We became very quiet, wondering just where Mama would go. My sister Bea thought maybe Africa. I thought of China. Again, I wished her ship would come in, real quick. Then she wouldn't think of going away.

Not very long after that, Mama did have a chance to go away on a vacation. A relative invited her to spend a week at a cottage on Cape Cod for a rest. That wasn't so very far, but at least it was a week away from us.

She hated every minute of it. In fact, she came back a day early, hugging and kissing each one of us again and again. She said, "Oh! I'm so glad to get back. I missed you so. I missed everything. I feel like getting down and kissing the floor. I'll never go away again."

We heard afterward that she had not been a very good houseguest, that she had worried about all of us, and wondered every minute what we were doing.

She missed the evening paper, she missed her favorite store, she missed the mailman. She might just as well have been on a faraway island, as she complained that it was too isolated. She longed to get back to "civilization."

After we grew up and got married, and went back home to visit, we would often tease Mama about the time she wanted to get away so far that we couldn't even send a penny postcard.

She would get very embarrassed and say, "Well, it's no wonder. There were days when you were little that I wanted to climb the walls. But," she added, "you were never really bad, but very lovable children."

In the golden years of Mama's life, I feel that her ship really did come in. Of course I know now that the phrase as spoken was part truth and part fantasy. She had dreams, desires, and yearnings, and she knew that one day at least some of them would be realized — her ship would come in.

It was her way of expressing her faith, her way of letting us know that she believed a better way of life would be forthcoming in the future, her way of saying, "Watch for the rainbow after the rain."

In the last years of her life, she was happy and content, all her needs and wants attended to with tender, loving care. Surely, no ship could hold a better cargo than that.

Fond Memories of "Old Doc"

TIME BRINGS CHANGES. AND IN FEW OTHER AREAS OF our lives is it as noticeable as it is when we need a physician.

In the old days, when I was a child, we did one of two things. Either we ran a few blocks around the corner to have our needs attended to personally, or one of us was sent to "fetch" the doctor to care for the ailing person. We knew him only as "Old Doc," but we had the greatest respect for him.

Now I realize that he was not old at all by our standards today; perhaps he was in his early sixties. His hair was silvery gray, his clothes shabby, but his eyes were bright and twinkling, and his hands quick and sure.

I don't ever recall him being too busy to come if the case was urgent. And I don't remember that anyone was ever turned away, even though the ailment might be a trivial one. Appointments were unheard of, as there were no telephones. At least we had none. There might be a few people ahead of us when we arrived, but we took seats and waited. Office hours were usually from 1 to 5 P.M. and 7 to 9 P.M. That meant that the doctor's visiting hours must be very early in the morning and very late at night. It was a common thing for him to work sixteen hours a day.

The doctor of the old days was not only a physician; he was a psychologist, a druggist, a spiritual advisor, a marriage counselor, and often a baby-sitter if a mother was too ill to care for her child during a visit. People had nowhere else to go with their problems.

For our family, at least, he was a dentist also. If anyone of us had a loose tooth, Papa pulled it out with pliers if he could. But if the job was too much for him, we were sent to Old Doc, often late at night when our parents couldn't stand our howling any longer. The price was twenty-five cents for one tooth; but Mother, who had "saving graces," usually sent two of us with forty cents to get a real bargain. We were given a sniff of ether or chloroform from a great horn, and out came the tooth.

Later, this horn was replaced by a huge ether dispenser on legs, and still later by an oxygen tank. We children looked at this fearful contraption in great awe and would not step within three feet of it. In the deepening gloom of the afternoon, it looked like some vicious creature from another world, ready to crush us with its long tubes and metal prongs.

Doc considered himself lucky to receive cash in any amount for his labors, as many of his patients had to pay in "goods"—chickens, eggs, garden stuff, or whatever they had to offer. Sometimes they paid in services: a new dress for Doc's wife, some shoes cobbled, repairs on his house, yard work, and so on. But often, too often, he received nothing at all, his only reward being the rehabilitation of his patients.

Doc traveled mostly with horse and buggy, but he walked a great deal also, often running a mile or more if he was needed in great haste. It was quicker than hitching up the buggy. When the last baby in our family was born, we had just moved to another house and there were boxes, barrels, and cartons all over the place.

"Run for the doc," said Mother, "and quick." I did, and he came running down the street behind me. The baby was born without incident, and by late afternoon and suppertime a young helper (a young woman of twenty-two years or so) was not only caring for us children, but for Mother and baby as well, besides cooking our supper and uncrating the boxes and barrels and putting the house in order quickly. She worked for her board and room, but gave us tender care, and we loved her. She was considered an "old maid" but was glad to get work.

Doc always had his pockets filled with peppermints and hard candies for his small patients, and he dispensed sugar pills by the hundreds for those little ailments for which there was no cure. In the long, cold winter months, boys were often sewed into their underwear, and Doc had to do a ripping job before they could be examined. Mothers didn't worry much then about sanitation. It was too cold to bathe often. Doc always sewed the garments back on again before they went home. And gave them candy for the trouble they had been through.

Medicines were not only prescribed by the doctor but must be furnished by him also. Drugstores were few and far between. His big black bag was loaded to the splitting point. My mother often mended it for him and, indeed, often sewed loose buttons on his coat or patched a little hole in his shirt. His own wife was too busy tending the sick and needy herself to give much time to these things.

I recall the time my older brother was brought home from the neighborhood skating pond. Someone had knocked him down accidentally, and stepped on his nose with sharp skates. His nose was practically falling off. I ran for Old Doc. He must have done an outstanding job, for not even a tiny scar remained, just a slight discoloration.

There was the day he took out my little sister's tonsils right on the kitchen table. His little daughter, only about eleven years old at the time, helped him — handing him things he needed. She was a real pro. She poured ether on half an orange, and held it to Sister's nose until she passed out. Then he went to work. After it was all over, he stayed to help clean up and to soothe little Sister when she awoke.

Doc always wore a frayed blue shop coat when he worked. I thought of this coat recently when I visited an orthodontist who was all dressed up in a shocking pink smock, blue satiny pants, and pink rubber gloves. I doubt that Doc owned any rubber gloves. I do know that he kept a big bar of yellow "Bee" soap in a wash basin by the sink, and no doubt he treated himself to a good scrub once in a while.

At school-opening time, Doc was very much in demand for vaccinations. We stood in assembly line with rolled-up sleeves. Ping! A shrill shriek, and it was over. Certainly it must have been very crude, since I still carry a scar as big as a silver dollar on my arm, as do most of my contemporaries. They didn't believe in hiding it then.

Once Old Doc took me to Boston with him to collect some pills. I recall that the round-trip trolley fare (from Worcester to Boston) was ninety cents for him and nothing for me, though I must have been over ten years of age at the time. We stopped at a drugstore before we came home and spent the remaining ten cents for two big dishes of ice cream. All the way home he pointed out places of interest through the car window. It was a memorable day in my life.

Every family had one or more aged people (seventy was considered aged then), and our family was no exception. We had both Grandma and Grandpa. It was not a custom of those days to be too solicitous of these old people. If they were washed, fed, and clothed, there duty and obligation ended. There were no periodic checkups as there are now. But Doc liked old folks and liked a family that was good to them. He never failed to inquire as to their health and to dispense a few pills or a laxative or tonic. They looked forward to his visits eagerly and anticipated his little treats as much as the children did.

Doctors in those days often had to make quick decisions and without consultations. When a neighbor's little girl was choking to death with membranous croup, unable to obtain enough oxygen through her lungs, Old Doc operated quickly and silently in the early hours of the morning on a cold winter night. The next night, the little girl might be pleading to go out to play.

Some of the complaints he received on a call were ridiculous. "Willie fell off the pianna. Come see if his arm is broken." If it wasn't, they certainly didn't think he should get paid for the call. Or "Grandma drunk up a whole bottle of Peruna, and she's awful sick." Or "Pa tied a black thread on his wart, and it's bleedin' awful." Or "Johnnie stuck his head in a chamber pot, and can't get it out." These and many other incidents bugged his life, but laughable or not, they had to be taken care of.

The memory of Doc's office is clearly etched in my mind. A desk littered with advertising pamphlets, bottles, and boxes, except for one corner reserved for his feet in the few leisurely moments he had. A row of battered chairs with broken cane seats. Two tall racks with many hooks for holding umbrellas with broken ribs and knobby, curved wooden handles.

Then there were many dusty, torn books for the

children to look at: *Mother Goose, Aesop's Fables, Anderson's Fairy Tales, The Bunny Family,* and so on. Books, too, for the adults to read. Lurid paper novels for the women, Police Gazettes for the men, and nickel "redbacks" and "Burlie" magazines, which I loved. They were so colorful. At one wall, a long, shiny horsehair couch for examinations. On a table, jars of tongue depressors and cloudy bottles of pills.

The doctor had no staff, so it was up to him to help a lady undress and hang up her voluminous petticoats. Then, after the examination was over, he had to help her get reassembled. If she had brought any little ones along, it was up to him to look after them too while she got dressed. It was not unusual for him to administer a good spanking if it was needed. He could do that too.

Then, just as now, many of the people who came to Old Doc's office were not really physically ill. They were troubled, they were lonely, they needed sympathy; life had become too much for them. But I never knew him to speak a harsh word, or to turn anyone away in anger, though he must have known many of the pains were ephemeral, temporary, or not at all serious.

I was happy to learn not long ago that his last days were spent in peaceful surroundings with people who loved him; that children visited him often to the time of his death. It must have been difficult for him not to prescribe for them if they complained at all of illness. But I'm sure the peppermints and sugar pills must have been forthcoming, at any rate.

Headphones and Belly Laughs

I'LL ALWAYS REMEMBER THE FIRST RADIO I EVER HEARD. My husband made it from a kit. It was a crude little thing, but we were enchanted. Oh! the pleasure we received from it. Headphones clamped close to our ears, we were in a world of our own. It was a wonderful world, alive with promise, in which anything and everything was possible.

Today, a radio is something teenagers carry around with them—often a little box no larger than four or five inches, which emits strange, discordant sounds. How different it was when we were young, back in the thirties and forties, when leisure hours were built around it. Magicians, earthshaking drama, the funniest of comedians, and adventure to chill and thrill the very marrow of one's bones came pouring from the speaker. The visual scenes had to be supplied from our own vivid imaginations.

As for size, our family radio was as tall as a washing machine, and just about as wide. Made of slick polished wood, it was the best-looking piece of furniture in the house. When the dial was turned, it made a hum which sounded like a motor. Then, after a few seconds, a voice would come in loud and clear: "You are listening to Radio WDBH." Ah . . . that was entertainment. We often sat up to the wee hours of the morning tuning into different stations. The first time we got Chicago, we were wild with excitement.

There was a special lure to those old-time radio shows. I wish I could go back, for just about one hour, lie on my back on the old wicker divan, with my eyes closed, my mind open, and listen once more to my old favorites. Television has much to offer, but there seems to be something missing—perhaps not enough use of our own imaginations.

Each member of the family had his or her own special interest, and it was an unwritten law that the time for that special spot should not be interfered with. There were arguments, of course, but they were always settled. The truth was, we loved to listen to anything. And the kids weren't the only ones; there was a time, in the early evening, when you could stroll down a quiet suburban street and hear the same programs drifting from almost every house—Lowell Thomas, the news commentator, Amos and Andy, the Goldbergs, and Mert and Marge.

And, in the daytime, from every house, every filling station, and every diner, there boomed the exciting, unmistakable, raspy voice of Boston's Fred

Hooey, whom *Variety* (the show business paper) once called "the greatest sports announcer in the country."

Remember "The Shadow" . . . that creaking door? Those famous words, "The seed of crime bears bitter, bitter fruit"? "Inner Sanctum" gave out chills when the announcer remarked in deep and solemn tones, "Dark, dark days are ahead of the doer of evil deeds." You had to believe him, and you couldn't wait for the next episode.

Remember the elephant graveyard in "Jack Armstrong"? He was the All-American Boy. Elephants, we were thrilled to learn, were wise and mysterious animals, who always knew when they were about to die. We sat in a trance while the stories of sacred cathedrals and stolen ivory unfolded. It happened in Africa, but our living room seemed filled with animals.

"Don Winslow of the Navy" had a special spot. "Buck Rogers," of course, and "The Lone Ranger" with his "Hi-yo Silver" echoed in our living room. And the comics . . . oh, what belly laughs they gave us. When Fibber McGee went into his closet and all the contents came tumbling out, we went into hysterics. When Amos and Andy went into their spiel, "Buzz me, Miss Blue," we rolled on the floor. How we laughed over their quarrels and predicaments. Nothing has ever equaled it.

"Gangbusters" was a noisy one, with screeching tires and machine guns; "Og, Son of Fire," for the science minded; "Mr. Keen, Tracer of Lost Persons"; "Sergeant Preston of the Yukon." And for the children, "Little Nemo," "Little Orphan Annie," "Skippy," and many more. Then, when the children went to bed, it was listening time for adults. Lux Radio Theatre from Hollywood with Cecil DeMille gave us wonderful entertainment with sound effects so vivid that we often crouched in terror.

There was Edgar Bergen with Charlie McCarthy — even if you couldn't see them, they were very funny. Fred Allen and all his comical characters of "Allen's Alley" came alive through the radio; Milton Berle with his songs and clowning; Eddie Cantor and Parkyakarkas. Kate Smith sang her lovely songs. I remember her theme song, "When the Moon Comes Over the Mountain." Jack Benny was in his heyday, then, and a favorite of us all.

There were fake feuds, too, that kept us laughing, between Bing Crosby and Bob Hope; Walter Winchell and "the old maestro," Ben Bernie. I remember the day that Orson Welles, with a simulated program, convinced millions of sober people that the earth had been invaded by Mars, and crowds fled panic-stricken through the streets. There were even some suicides. That's how realistic radio was.

Of course, there are similarities between radio and television, but there are differences, too, mostly in the announcers. They seemed like friends you almost knew personally, men from all walks of life who brought their individuality with them. There were none of the homogenized accents and mannerisms we hear on television today.

Even during station breaks, the announcers' voices were as individual as a trademark on a bar of soap: Norman Brokenshire, Ford Bond, Graham McNamee, Ben Grauer, Hugh James, George Hicks, Bob Trout, Ken Carpenter, Don Wilson, and Pierre André. Those were some of the big ones.

Saturday afternoon was opera time, and that was when I first learned of its delights: *Il Trovatore* and *Lucia di Lammermoor, Madame Butterfly* (which enchanted me), *The Barber of Seville.* I heard Caruso and Melba and Galli-Curci. Much of it was recorded, but it instilled in me a love of good music that has stayed with me through the years.

And, then, quite often, a thrilling surprise: from a famous nightclub, live, amid the tinkle of china and women's laughter, came the voice of the announcer: "Ladies and gentlemen—direct from the Aragon Paragon Ballroom on Chicago's North Side"; "Direct from the Glen Island Casino," or "From Frank Daily's famous Meadowbrook—we present . . ."

Some of the names appearing at these places were Les Brown and his Band of Renown, Joe Rines from the Mayfair in Boston, Dol Brissette from the Roof Gardens of Hotel Bancroft in Worcester, Vaughn Monroe from the beautiful Terrace dining room of the Hotel Statler in downtown Boston, Tony Pastor, Artie Shaw, Benny Goodman.

It was a simpler day, I suppose. Perhaps we were more easily satisfied. But all those enchanted hours are locked in my heart: all the wonderful shows, the wonderful men and women who entertained us; all the fear and suspense, all the nonsense, and all the dreamy hours. Good-bye, old-time radio.

Grandma's Album

THE COMPLEX FABRIC OF MEMORY OFTEN UNCOVERS IN-cidents and objects connected with our youth, and brings them back with astonishing clarity. To me, just the mention of Christmas brings to my mind the heavy volume that was Grandma's Christmas album.

Every year, about mid-November, it was brought out from its hiding place so that Grandma might plan our Christmas. When we children saw the album, we knew Christmas was very, very close. The cover was of bright red, soft leatherlike material. At each corner, angels were painted, white ones with golden wings, and in the center, in golden script, were the words,

All things bright and beautiful
All creatures great and small
All things wise and wonderful
The good Lord made them all.

The cover was beautiful, but inside, the pages were worn and shabby. The last time I saw it, some of them were crumbling with age. Many of the pages were filled with recipes that had been clipped from newspapers and women's magazines, and some handwritten in the flowing script of the day. Pages and pages of cakes and cookies, pies and puddings, stews and roasts. "Fireman's Stew" and "Monday Pudding" are still favorites, with perhaps a few changes to modern ingredients.

But the cooking "rules" were only a small part of the album. There were clippings of lovely poems of Christmastime, and beautiful lines from classics such as "The Snow Shower" by William Cullen Bryant, "The Oriole's Nest," and "God Knows Best." Every child, large or small, was expected to take part in entertaining on Christmas afternoon after the big dinner.

There were pages of presents. It seems the word *gift* was not used very much. You gave a present on Christmas Day, and all the presents were homemade. There were descriptions of handkerchief boxes of cardboard covered with material—often satin and lace. Dainty corset covers, pincushions, embroidered picture frames, pillows in many shapes, aprons of many kinds. And for the children to make—pen wipers of flannelette tied with pretty ribbons, bookmarks, samplers, and doilies.

Quite a large section of the album was devoted to homemade remedies. For many of the Christmas gifts were meant to help people. Grandma was known for her nursing ability. She was a friend in need to all her neighbors. Her cupboards were stocked with homemade remedies, and she seemed to always know which one to reach for, instinctively. Often, on languid summer days she would go out into the fields to gather herbs with which to make her salves, lotions, and potions.

And here in the album were all the "receipts" for those healing remedies. One called for roots such as mandrake, elder, and bloodroot to be boiled for many hours, then mashed, strained, and mixed with other ingredients to form a soft white salve with a pinkish glow. It was used for fever sores, chilblains (with which we children were sorely troubled), and various aches and pains. Very healing it was.

There were rules for syrups for coughs and colds — garlic, honey, glycerine, molasses, peppermint. There was balm-of-Gilead for chapped hands, and a brew of hemlock bark for diarrhea. A salve made of horse-radish root for neuralgia and toothache, strong enough to make one forget the pain. A rubbing compound too, made of a weird mixture of tobacco leaf, arnica, and snuff, marked "very effective."

Grandma received no reward for all her labors. She said it gave her a good feeling to be able to help others. While we were busy making Christmas gifts, Grandma was busy with her herbs, little jars and bottles all around her, brewing and mashing, making up these thoughtful presents for her neighbors.

There was one whole section devoted to cosmetics. Yes, Grandma made her own. Lotions of rose water and glycerine; powder of starch and talcum with perfume of dried rose leaves. Shampoos of homemade soap and fragrant oils. Shave lotions with sweet oil and geranium leaves boiled together, then strained. All these were made for Christmas gifts for both men and women.

There were pages for dyes made from roots, onion skins, beets, sumac berries, goldenrod, butternut bark, gallberry leaves, and many other things. Grandma used these dyes to color her rag strips for rugs, and for her curtains and spreads, often made of flour bags. And she bottled some for presents. No one would think of giving these things today, but in those days of no "five and dime," they were indeed welcome.

She made wines for giving also, and a few of the pages were given over to this. She brewed mead, "the drink of the gods," and elderberry wine from the blossoms, which were plentiful—even goldenrod wine and chokecherry wine. She made light soft drinks from sassafras, birch bark, and juniper berries. And tea from raspberry leaves and other berry leaves, for real tea was hard to come by and very expensive.

She said she learned a great deal from her own grandmother, who in turn had learned much from the Indians. The Indians, her grandmother told her, always picked herbs, each in the right phase of the moon. They used a great deal of tansy, she told her, and so Grandma, too, thought there was nothing in the world like tansy for that "all-gone feeling." (It was also good for the liver.) And in the spring, we all had to take a dose with sulfur, and the taste was horrible.

An important part of Grandma's album consisted of two heavy pages glued together to form a pocket. In here were placed the poems and drawings by the children (and a few by grownups, too). On the cover of the pocket were the words, "Family Fun. At Christmastime." The only rule was that everything must be original.

There were many silly little poems such as this one by "Little Bee":

> *Christmas is here*
> *For Goodness' sake.*
> *And I know I'll have*
> *A belly ache.*

And there were many pictures, crude drawings, colored with Grandma's dyes, for crayons, too, were hard to come by. One, quite good, must have been done by a grownup. It pictured Uncle Jake with his corncob pipe in one hand, and in the other, a violently colored necktie which he regarded with a mixed expression of delight and woe. There was a sad little picture of my little sister Nell, who died in the fall of the year. Underneath it were the words of a then-popular song, "I'm tying the leaves so they won't come down, so Nellie won't go away." Grandma and Mother both cried whenever that pocket of the album was opened.

All the contents of Grandma's album prove her

wonderful homemaking abilities, her wisdom, her love for her family, and her way of life. We know that life was hard for her, but it was not dull. The little pleasures and excitements of her life meant just as much to her as ours do today—perhaps even more. And many of our cares and worries she did not have. I doubt that she even knew the meaning of the word *psychoanalysis.* She just did her best, day by day, and placed her faith in God. And I often wish, while trying out some of Grandma's "rules," that I could acquire some of the serenity which made her the lovely and remarkable person whom we remember so well.

When April Was Auction Month

Lay it where dreams are twined,
In memory's mystic land.

—LEWIS CARROLL

THE SAP IN THE MAPLES HAD COME AND GONE, THE WILD geese were on their way north, and so were the snow-birds, the sunshine seekers. It was April, and in the old days, this was auction time. There were no flea markets then, and no yard sales, but auctions were numerous, especially in New England. People flocked to them from far and wide, on foot, by horse and buggy, or on horseback. Some came to purchase, some for excitement, and some just out of curiosity. There were the old, the young, barefoot children, and lovers hand in hand.

Some of the men came dressed in Burberry coats and top hats, and some came in ragged overalls. There were ladies in silk dresses and straw hats covered with flowers, and others with smelly dark cotton dresses worn to swill the pigs. There were children with snow-white pinafores and patent leather shoes, and children with patched breeches and dirty faces.

Down from the attic would come spinning wheels, yarn winders, rheumatic Boston rockers with sagging seats or no seats at all; horsehair divans, shiny and prickly; "Sandwich" glass sauce dishes (nee Woolworth), dusty and chipped, at least ten years old, but now rated as antiques; flyspecked Currier and Ives prints, and Maxfield Parrish pictures in tarnished frames.

Hooked rugs with the patina that settles on them after ten years of supplying a route between the kitchen and the barn were given a shake or two, and thrown over chair backs. (Nothing "antiques" quicker than a hooked rug.) Patchwork quilts were here too, hung up on a clothesline with all the memories sewn into them, containing scraps of Grandma's wedding dress, Grandpa's velvet house jacket, and Aunt Rilla's paisley shawl. And oh! so difficult to part with.

Smaller pieces would be piled on a table. There would be those little glass plates called "cup-plates," used by our dainty ancestors who drank very hot tea from a saucer, and had to have a place to rest the cup, so as not to soil the snowy linen cloth. And surely there would be a few dark blue plates with historic views of early America on them, which were brought in great quantity from England, became very popular, then were discarded in favor of daintier china of Bristol and Old Worcester, and were banished to the attic and called "poor man's china."

And there would surely be many fat bottles with profiles of our country's patriots engraved on them, perhaps even one with "The Father of Our Country," in which to store teeth and whatnot. And many items of tin, boxes and trays with brushes and stencils for decorating. And most probably a few luster pitchers, mostly chipped, but still beautiful with glints of silver and gold and copper.

Souvenir items were plentiful, many brought home from the Centennial Fair of 1876 or the World's Fair of 1893. There were ashtrays with pictures of the fair on them, vases and mirrors and pincushions, combs and hair receivers, plates and pickle boats and china cups and saucers. All of these items sold very cheap at the time of the fairs, but today are priced at quite a high sum.

At these old country auctions, bidding was always slow, and most items went at a ridiculously low price. It was not uncommon to see a beautiful highboy dresser go for as little as $30 or $40. Or a mahogany table for $25. Or a Tiffany lamp for $15 or less. At one auction in the town of West Boylston some fifty years ago, a complete bedroom set of mahogany with four-poster bed, dressers and chairs, and springs and mattress sold for $30, the highest bid.

At this same auction, the complete furnishings of a 10-room Colonial house were spread out on the wide green lawn. Many lovely dishes were almost given away, and I acquired several historic Staffordshire plates for 25 cents each. And a lovely Maxfield Parrish print (*Country Garden*) for 35 cents. There were many cartons of books here, too. Always on the lookout for books I could get a story from, I had seen a book in one carton that I had heard a lot about: *Dr. Hunter's Family Advisor.* This book recommended ointment made of boiled toads for rheumatism, and a swallow of kerosene for a common cold. I wanted that book, and made a mental note to bid as high as two dollars for it. The bidding stopped at a dollar and a half, and I was stunned when the auctioneer said, "Sold! To the woman in a red hat, all the books on the lawn." I had bought the complete library, almost a thousand books. It took my husband, myself, and my son three hours to haul the books to our home a half-mile away. I had shelves made up in the barn loft for them, and had reading on hand for years to come.

I recall another April auction vividly, because of an incident that was a near tragedy. Chamber pots were a very popular item at these country auctions. While some were of plain white earthenware, many were made of English porcelain china, and beautifully decorated. A small boy, perhaps eight or nine years old, was feeling mischievous and had taken one of these chamber pots, a smallish one, and shoved it down over his head. He ran around and clowned, and everyone laughed; it was very funny. But when he attempted to remove it, it was not funny anymore.

Though he twisted it and turned it desperately, he could not get it any higher than his chin. Grownups rushed to help him, with no success. He became limp, and sank to the ground.

By this time a crowd had gathered round, the bidding stopped, and the auctioneer knew something was wrong. He ran to the boy. "I've got to do something drastic," he said, "or this boy will strangle to death." He lifted his heavy gavel, and brought it down hard on the chamber pot. But the pot was evidently very hard for it only cracked slightly. The auctioneer lifted the gavel again, much higher, and gave the pot a fierce blow. The boy let out a loud cry of pain and became unconscious, but the pot broke in half and fell to the ground. The poor little boy was nearly dead, but the fresh air revived him. He was carried home, and soon was well again, but it was a close call.

The children in the neighborhood made up a song, to the tune of "Yankee Doodle," that was sung for quite a while afterward,

> *Don't put a chamber pot on your head;*
> *Your head is big and bony;*
> *Put the chamber pot under the bed*
> *And call it macaroni.*

That Old Gypsy Mystique

WHERE HAVE THE GYPSIES GONE? I REMEMBER THEM with such delight. At the turn of the century, they would suddenly appear in our town in great numbers, usually in March or April. They arrived in bright caravans, loaded down with utensils and bedding, squawking chickens, baskets, and burlap bags of food. The wagons creaked and swayed as they rolled by our home to camp in a field nearby.

I remember the men with bright bandanas on their heads, up high in the front seats of the wagons, the women inside wearing voluminous skirts of bright cottons, gay kerchiefs on their heads, and dangling hoops of gold in their ears. Young girls sat in the rear of the wagons, their golden legs swinging up and down. Barefoot, ragged children tagged along behind the caravan.

And, as clearly as though it happened yesterday, I remember one night when we four children were alone in the house. My oldest sister, who was thirteen, was in charge. I was eight. Our parents had gone to visit a sick friend, and before leaving we were given strict orders: "Lock the doors! Don't let anyone in unless you are very sure who it is." This was most unusual. We were a family without fear, running in and out of doors, which were open at all hours.

But something had happened that day. The gypsies had come to town! Year after year they came, to camp in every available empty lot, over the objections of the community and in spite of the rulings and edicts of the city fathers. Each year, as they arrived, the rumors would start, and then spread. The women whispered over the back fences, and we children hid behind shrubs to listen.

"Remember last year—the little Fenton girl was missing! You know she had jet black hair and blue eyes. That's the kind they like." Having black hair and blue eyes myself, I shivered with fear, and vowed they would never get me. I was terrified . . . that is, until I met Molly Faw.

On that particular night, we were all sitting around the table playing Chinese checkers. Suddenly, there was a sharp rap at the door. "Who's there?" my sister called out. There was no answer. I started to cry. My brother, who considered himself my protector, frightened me more by assuring me that "those old gypsies" would never get me.

He started to push heavy articles against the door, and we huddled together in the furthest corner of the room, too scared to play our game. All was quiet, but we knew, we were sure, that someone was out there.

An hour or so later, our parents came home. Hearing their voices, we removed the objects and opened the door. There, on the mat, curled up in sleep, was a little girl about my own age. She was shabbily but colorfully dressed. Her face was dirty and tear-stained. Mother woke her gently.

"What is your name," Mother asked, "and why are you here?" She hung her head. "I am Molly Faw," she answered, as she started to cry. "I was picking up wood for our fire and I got losted." She had a queer accent, and I could barely understand her. Mother told Papa to get the police, and while he was gone, she washed Molly's face and fed her bread and milk.

We saw now that she was very pretty, and, after her repast, she became very talkative. Though her accent was queer, and some of her words were unintelligible, she smiled a lot, and quickly we became the best of friends. Soon, the police came to take her back to her people. I felt very lonely after she had gone.

The next day, we found out that the gypsy camp was not too far from our home. Molly often came by the house, and we would talk and play in the yard while her mother went around the neighborhood selling baskets. Molly taught me how to weave little baskets and make dolls from cornhusks. She also taught me many little songs and dances.

One day, she told me there was to be a wedding that night. "Can't you come?" she asked. "It will be real perty, and moochy music and dancing. And moochy good tings to eat." She swirled around and around. "We be dancin' all the night. You be comin'."

I knew I would not be allowed to go, if I asked permission, so I persuaded my brother to accompany me. We stole out of the house as soon as it got dark. Molly had promised to watch for us. When we reached the meadow, she was there. She led us to the edge of the campgrounds, and told us to wait, seated on a stone wall.

I could see the dark tents and the caravans, and red lanterns hung on poles. A flickering circle of light illuminated the many forms milling around, lighting fires, laying blankets on the ground, carrying food to tables. The brightness of their clothes made the scene appear like a giant patchwork quilt suddenly come alive. There were shouts, good-natured curses, and a great deal of laughter.

Suddenly, there was a hush and I heard the strains of a violin . . . not a sound was heard except the plaintive, gentle music. Then, a shout: "Here they come." Out of the largest tent came the wedding pair. She was dressed in a bright orange skirt, yards and yards of material swirling about her. She wore bangles in her ears and on her arms, and bright streamers flowed from her hair, which was jet black and hanging to her waist.

He wore tight black pants and a bright orange silk blouse. He, too, had bangles in his ears, and gold chains around his neck. Each held one end of an orange scarf, about two feet long, and they swung it as they walked.

"Her name is Marcy," said Molly, who had come to sit with us, "and his name is Tamus. Tamus Bailey." Then she added. "They are in love, and they are goin' to have twelve childer."

Soon, a large wooden bowl was brought out, the bridal pair drank from it, and it was passed to all the others. After the last one had sipped, it was brought to us, and we, too, sipped from it.

Now, the couple kissed, and the orange scarf was wound about their necks. The violin played again. "But they are not married yet," said Molly. "They must first embrace the horse." Sure enough, a beautiful black horse was brought out to stand before them. "The horse is their wedding present," said Molly, "and if they separate, the horse will save them." They embraced the horse, then embraced each other once more. Then they were led back into the tent and the singing and dancing began.

Molly led us into the gay, whirling group, and we danced with them. Later, much later, when the women started to spread out the food for the feast, we knew we had to leave. Quickly, we ran home. We had not been missed, and I dared not tell. I had to keep secret one of the most joyous evenings of my life. All night, I fancied I could hear the gypsies dancing and singing. To this day, I can see them, a lovely secret episode I shall always have in my gallery of memories.

Where did they come from, these people who set themselves apart? And where are they now? There are various stories about their origin; most trace them back to India. The word *gypsy* is a corruption of *Egyptian*, from where they were believed to have emigrated in the fourteenth or fifteenth century. Trekking into Europe, they settled in large bands in Scotland, France, England, Spain, and, much later of course, America. They were not allowed in Sweden, and in the Netherlands they were excluded under pain of death by decree of Charles V, in 1582.

Those coming to the United States were mostly tribes banished from England and Scotland. Many came after the Revolution. They formed bands and roamed as nomads, staying in one place until they were chased away. But in New England, they soon became semisettled, following itinerant occupations. They became, more or less, tinkers, or jacks-of-all-trades: peddlers, tinsmiths, horse traders, and the like.

Later, they became musicians, singing waiters, and tavern keepers. The women wove baskets, peddling them around to homes as they told the fortunes of the housewives: "Cross my palm with silver, lydie, and I will tell a good, true fortune." By 1892, the patterns and behavior of the gypsies had begun to change. The tent gypsies began to seek the shelter and warmth of abandoned buildings.

Their reputation, based somewhat on truth but blown up by rumor and old wives' tales, was so unsavory that the people put up a great fuss and cry. They were accused of horse stealing, chicken stealing, even child stealing. Every calamity that befell the community was laid to them—fires, smallpox, accidents, even deaths, for many people believed they practiced witchcraft.

In many towns the people rose up and issued edicts against them, but it was deemed unfair by some who had good relations with them.

There was an aura of romance about the gypsies that captured the fancy of many. In 1891 J. M. Barrie's book *The Little Minister* was published, and it helped to foster that romance. Through the years, there were many songs to keep it alive. And the gypsy music was so hauntingly lovely! Franz Liszt, the composer, once said that all Hungarian music originated with the gypsies.

Where have they gone, these nomads of a bygone day? Surely there are some still here. The mechanic who serviced your car, perhaps; the man who came to pick up your clothes for the cleaners; the waitress who served you in that little café; the man who drives the bus going down the street where you live. Any one of them could be a gypsy. And, if the name is Fay, Faa, or Faw, or Bailey, Balee, or Bailee, there's more than a chance that he might well be.

The modern way of life and the advent of the automobile have forced changes in their way of living. The old traditions and beliefs, out of necessity, have been pushed into the background. But, wherever they are, and whoever they are, there is a yearning for the old way of life, their hearts surely beat faster whenever they hear the wind sighing in the trees, look out upon a moonlit night, see smoke curling up from a distant hill—or hear the sweet strains of a violin playing a haunting gypsy melody.

Hard Times Come Knocking

WE DIDN'T SEE MUCH OF PAPA WHEN WE WERE SMALL.
He worked long hours at an iron foundry, from six in
the morning to six at night. When he came home, he
washed up, ate his supper, and went to bed.

Except on Saturdays. On Saturdays he came home
at noon. After dinner, he helped with the housework,
beating the rugs, washing the kitchen linoleum, pol-
ishing the furniture. Then he bathed, and dressed in
his best. For this was Papa's weekly holiday. I thought
Papa looked very handsome, in his charcoal-colored
double-breasted jacket and pinstriped pants. He was
not tall, perhaps about five foot seven, but his slender-
ness made him look taller. He had fair skin, with a
pink flush in his cheeks, and a little black mustache,
which he twisted upwards. He parted his black hair
smartly and neatly in the middle. His teeth were small
and white, and he had a lovely smile.

On Saturdays, one of his comrades called for him,
perhaps with horse and buggy. Sometimes they took
the trolley car that went right by the house. At the

foundry Papa was a special pattern molder, designing things for others to copy. He was paid a twenty-dollar gold piece and a silver dollar every Saturday. This was considered quite high wages for the times. When he left for his half-day holiday, he took the gold and the dollar in his wallet. "But it's only for show, Mama, it will always come back to you," he would say. "I will spend only the dollar."

But Mama worried. She always stayed up and waited for him to come home. She was afraid he might lose it, or it might be stolen from him. And once it was. Papa opened his wallet to give her the gold, and the wallet was empty but for a few dimes and pennies. He couldn't believe it. He emptied it inside out and outside in. No gold. Needless to say, Mama and Papa slept little that night.

The next morning Mama called the café where Papa had met his friends. No one had seen the gold. But soon afterwards our doorbell rang, and a young boy stood there with a small package. In it was the gold piece. It had been found by the manager, on the chair where Papa sat. He knew Papa always carried a twenty-dollar gold piece. And he sent the boy as soon as he could. Mama gave the boy a dollar, and he was overjoyed. He did not know what he had been carrying.

Every noon it was my task to carry Papa's dinner to him at the foundry. It was a task I loved. Papa had no time to come home, as he had only forty-five minutes' recess, and I had two hours. School recess was from twelve o'clock to two o'clock, so after I ate dinner, I still had plenty of time. It was so delightfully warm in the foundry, and I loved watching the flaming forges. The men called "Hello Missy" to me, and some of them would give me a cookie or a wrapped candy.

Mama took great pains with Papa's dinner. (We never used the word *lunch*. It was breakfast, dinner, and supper.) She put it up in a three-layer tin bucket with a sturdy wooden handle. First, in the bottom, a thick soup with croutons. In the middle container, whatever we had had for dinner—a chop, or a chicken leg, or a slice of meat with gravy, and a baked potato, generously buttered. And two thick slices of her home-baked bread, also generously buttered. In the top section, a piece of pie, or a square of cake, or a dish of pudding or custard. Then she tied a thick layer of newspapers around it to keep it hot. I carried a pint bottle of coffee in my cape pocket, also wrapped in newspaper. When Papa opened his pail and sniffed the contents, he always said "Ah! That *femme* of mine."

Sometimes Papa had a little gift for me—a tiny little iron frog, a flatiron, a little jug, an eagle, or some such thing. I kept these things for many years.

It was in October in the year 1904 that Papa complained of a sore throat, and we noticed that he didn't look good. His kind, gray eyes looked dull, his skin looked dry and gray, and his mustache drooped downward. Still, he kept working. But one morning, after rising, he fell back into bed. "Mama," he said, "I just cannot go to work this morning." Mama got the

doctor to come, and he reported that Papa was very ill
with rheumatic fever. "He must have complete bed
rest for at least a month. If not, it will affect his heart.
Maybe it already has. He should not have been
working."

After the doctor left, Mama gave Papa his breakfast, then covered him up warmly. "Don't you dare
try to get up," she said. "We are going to be just fine. I
have some savings. We won't go hungry. Now, don't
you worry. Just rest, go back to sleep." There was no
such thing as unemployment wages in those days, and
no health insurance. If you didn't work, you didn't
get paid, and that was it.

That evening, Mama called us all together. "Now,
children," she said, "there will be no money coming
in for a while. Papa is very ill. But if you all cooperate,
we will not go hungry, I promise you. I have saved
some money, and we have lots of good things in the
cellar cabinets. But there will be no more fudge making, no new clothes or shoes, no parties, and no
nickelodeons. And you must all help in every way you
can. If Papa gets well, I will make it all up to you."

And we did help. My brothers and sisters were
wonderful. Will got a paper route, and poured his
dimes in my hand every Saturday. He also sold *Saturday Evening Post*s at five cents each, and he could
keep one cent. As he had twenty-five customers, he
had an extra quarter to give me each week—enough
to buy flour for a week's supply of bread.

My sister Rose, who had a beautiful singing voice

and knew all the popular songs, sang at parties for twenty-five cents a performance. Little Bea sang too, and did a cute little dance to go with her songs. Her audiences loved her, and she loved being a performer. I baby-sat, and killed flies, and ran errands for the neighbors. Even the little boys, now two and three years old, helped, raking leaves and gathering apples, "to help Papa get well," they said.

When Papa's Bon-Ami Club sent a messenger with a gift of twenty-five dollars, Mama accepted it with tears and gratitude. We didn't want charity, but this was an organization to which Papa had always paid his dollar-a-month dues promptly. Mama used that money to stock the fuel bin with coal for the winter. Now, we knew we'd be warm. And Papa was slowly improving. The day came, late in November, when he sat in the chair by the window. And in a week or so, he was walking about the room. On Thanksgiving Day, he ate dinner with us, then went back to bed.

A week before Christmas, he went back to work. He was looking good. His eyes were bright, the pink flush back in his cheeks, his little mustache twisted upwards again. And with the ache gone from his legs, he had his jaunty walk back again.

We had a happy Christmas that year. Turkey and all the fixin's. We exchanged homemade gifts. For Papa I had bought a mustache cup at a church fair for ten of my hard-earned pennies, and painted the word *Papa* on it with gilt paint. He said it was the nicest thing he ever owned.

Mama made us all promise to say a prayer of thanks that night for Papa's recovery. And after dinner, she brought in a cake, frosted with snowy icing, and in red icing the words, "Welcome back, Papa, and Merry Christmas." Papa looked at it and said, "Ah!— That *femme*." Then he put his arms around it, and said, "You see, my name is on it! No one else can have any. I'm going to eat it all myself." We knew then that he was really well again, for he had gotten back to his old teasing ways.

Summers of Old

OH! THE SWEETNESS OF THOSE SUMMER DAYS IN THE early 1900s. When Mama allowed us to doff our long underwear and put on our sleeveless knit shirts, we knew summer had arrived. And when those early troubadours (then called "tramps") came knocking at our back doors for a handout, we knew that it was here for good. In June, the whole world seemed in tune. The first garden vegetables were ready for picking—the young onions, the little red radishes, the sweet green peas. The early strawberries were showing pink, and visions of luscious shortcake danced in our heads.

The fences around our yard were a mass of red and white rambling roses, blossoming in all their glory. Early green apples were begging to be made into pies and sauce. And the robins were feasting on the cherries, while we hastened to get our share.

We measured the seasons by the roadside flowers. In early spring there were violets and crab-apple blossoms, followed by daisies and buttercups; then black-eyed Susans, wild irises, and goldenrod, followed by blue-fringed gentian violets, at the time my favorite flower.

It was quiet in the streets in those days. Only the soft whir of the trolley cars passing by every half-hour, the clop-clop of the horses' hoofs, and the faint squeak of wagon wheels could be heard . . . the occasional song of a bird, and the *whish-whish* of katydids in the trees.

Our playhouse was the grapevine-covered trellis in the side yard. Here, we brought our dolls and home-made doll furniture on fair, summer days to set up housekeeping—a wooden box for a table, red bricks for a stove, broken bits of crockery and china, broken cookies and crackers. We played for hours, with various cousins and neighborhood children.

Sometimes, my brothers would take possession of the playhouse to play their cruel game of "horse-chestnut battle," which they were forbidden to play, for it was a dangerous game. Large horse chestnuts were strung on long, heavy strings, and these were held by opponents and hurled against each other, to see who could knock off the most chestnuts quickly. Very often, someone would get badly hurt, an eye injury or facial bruise. Then, too, they needed privacy to swap their baseball cards and cigarette silken flags, which were held in high esteem and required careful consideration.

There was a bright-colored woven hammock hanging in the backyard. This was one of my favorite haunts. Oh! The wonderful reading I did in that hammock. I read everything I could lay my hands on. We had a few books on our living-room shelves— *Aesop's Fables,* a set of Dickens that I read over and over. *The Old Curiosity Shop* was my favorite, and I cried each time I read it.

I had a library card when I was seven years old. My sister and I would walk the length of Main Street in Worcester to the library on Elm Street, passing the beautiful homes with lace-curtained windows, usually open, so we could see the lovely interiors.

The books I loved during those hammock days were the adventurous ones: anything of Jack London's, Kipling, *Robinson Crusoe, Robin Hood,* the *Arabian Nights, King Solomon's Mines,* all the Horatio Alger books, and all the fairy tales.

When I was about ten years old, I got hold of Elinor Glyn's *Three Weeks,* which was much talked about at that time. I hid it under my bed, but Mama found it. She didn't forbid me to read it, but said, "If you read trash, you'll be trash." I never finished it, and I've kept that sentence in my mind ever since.

Occasionally, my sisters and brothers would pry me from the hammock to play games on the quiet street. We played hopscotch, and a peculiar game called "Give Me a Bow," in which we accosted passersby to ask them for a bow, and wrote it down if we were accommodated. And there was jackstones and fortunetelling with the buttons on our clothes. "Rich man, poor man, beggar, thief—merchant, lawyer, doctor, chief" was yet another summer diversion. While the boys played marbles and mumbletypeg, we jumped rope to gay tunes.

After supper we would play under the gas lamps. Games that captured our attention included Run Sheepie Run, hide-and-seek, and blindman's bluff. And, if Papa had the hose out to water the garden, we would run in and out of the spray, shrieking with laughter . . . the street no longer quiet. We were happy, carefree children, in those sweet summer days of long ago.

Too Fat to Be an Angel

I WAS ABOUT NINE YEARS OLD, IN THE FOURTH GRADE, and very excited when teacher, Miss Graves, announced shortly after Thanksgiving in 1904 that we were going to put on a Christmas play.

My excitement rose to near frenzy when she told me I could be one of the angels. Mother was to make my angel robe of sheer white fabric and the wings were to be fashioned of cardboard painted white and covered with the white fabric.

Mother got started on it immediately and we fussed with measurements. Everything had to be just so. Wings, fourteen inches long and ten inches wide. Robe must reach exactly to the floor. Sleeves must come exactly to the waist. I was measured again and again. Every day after school we worked on the costume. The whole family was involved, searching for gold ribbons, white socks, slippers, and undergarments.

Every day, the teacher would send new directions and the costume would have to be changed a little.

Robe must have an elastic at the waist. Sleeves must cover fingers. Neckline must be very close, and other small things. Mother became weary of the whole thing and kept declaring that she would be glad when the play was over.

Then, just a week before the date, Miss Graves changed her plans. She set the date a few days later and she also changed the cast. I was stricken with horror, frustration, and disbelief when she announced that I was "out."

"I've changed my mind, Jenny, you're too fat to be an angel. I'll put you in another part."

"But," I cried, "the costume is almost done. My mother has worked so hard on it. What will she say?"

Miss Graves said, "Don't worry about it, I'll buy it from her for another little girl."

I was heartbroken and hated to go home that afternoon, knowing that I must break the news to my mother.

When I arrived home, I went into my bedroom and there was my beautiful robe hanging on the wall, all ready to put on. I sobbed my heart out. How could she do this to me? I was plump to be sure. But I wasn't that fat. Tommie Parker was fatter than me and he was going to be Joseph. It just wasn't fair. I didn't even want to be in the old play. If I couldn't be an angel, I didn't want to be anything.

But when I informed my mother, she took it very calmly. She said that perhaps now I would stop eating between meals and lose a little weight, although she loved me just as I was. Making the costume was a labor of love. They could have it free.

My father, however, did not take it so calmly. He was, in fact, furious.

"Too fat!" he yelled. "She is just right. Shows she gets enough to eat. I don't want her skinny."

Well, that made me feel better. He was angry about the robe, too. "Sure it was a labor of love. Love for you, no one else. And, by gum, I'm going to see that you wear it. I'll take an hour off and have a talk with that teacher."

The next day, he did stop and have a talk with Miss Graves. He told us all about it afterwards, with great glee. "She was all apologies," he said. She told him I had misunderstood her. "Jenny is going to have the leading role," she told him. "She has such a nice voice and she reads so well. I want her to be the narrator. And, of course, she can wear the robe; except the wings. She will not be an angel, but she will be seen. I am so sorry that she did not understand."

So Papa was happy. But I knew that it must have been a sudden decision, for she certainly had said nothing to me about being the narrator.

I had only a few days to read the text so that I would get it smoothly, but I loved to read aloud and I knew I'd have no trouble. I was overjoyed. The narration was very important and I was going to wear the lovely robe, after all. I knew that Miss Graves must have been holding that role for the right decision.

The evening for the play arrived—a beautiful, clear,

cold December night. A little light snow had fallen, just enough to cover the ground; it was a perfect night for the play. The school hall was bright with green garlands and red ribbons and every seat was taken. Many people were standing against the wall also. It seemed the whole neighborhood had turned out to see and hear our play.

We had no stage, just a raised platform where we assembled for exercise classes. All the kids were there, noisy and excited, waiting to be placed in order. The crib with the baby doll was in the center and in the background were a few life-sized animals of cardboard. Someone had thrown a little hay around to make it look more like a stable. The kids were all placed in order.

The lights went up a little brighter; that was my signal to begin. Then, something very funny happened, but it almost ruined the evening.

I started reading the beloved story, starting with the title, *There Was No Room at the Inn,* the story of the Holy Family. Suddenly, there was a loud explosion. No one had remembered that Tommie Parker, who was Joseph, suffered from hay fever. He gave out loud, whopping sneezes, one after another.

But Miss Graves was equal to the emergency. The lights dimmed. She ran onto the platform with a broom and quickly swept the hay from the floor. Tommie stopped sneezing, the lights went up, and once again I started my narration. From then on, everything went smoothly and beautifully.

The angels moved gracefully and went through all their lovely motions without a hitch. The three wise men came in and delivered their gifts, bowing and smiling. Mary sat by the crib, in a low chair, with her hands folded in her lap. Joseph knelt on one knee and kissed her hands.

I read on and on. The hall was very, very quiet. Even the small children were quiet, listening to every word. In less than half an hour, it was over. It was still very quiet. Many had tears in their eyes. Then suddenly, applause. Wonderful applause. And they all rose to come towards us.

The parents hugged their little performers. The praises came from everyone. "You were all wonderful." "It was so beautiful." "It was just perfect." My parents hugged me. "Jenny, you read so beautifully. You never stumbled once." I was indeed a proud and happy little girl.

Everyone went to the adjoining room for refreshments, but still talking and praising our performance. Of course everyone praised Miss Graves also and she surely deserved it. It was a lovely night in my life— one that I will never forget.

Those Fabulous Toys
of My Childhood

SOME FAMOUS MAN ONCE SAID, "IT IS MEMORY THAT gives width and breadth and deepness to a man's life. To keep his past alive is to increase his enjoyment of the present, and to some extent, to give fuller meaning to his future."

At Christmastime, my memories are of the Christmases of my childhood, and they focus on the wonderful toys we children received and shared. A few of these toys I still keep and cherish.

No doubt the origin of toys goes back to prehistoric times. The cave men probably carved animals of stone and wood to amuse their little ones, and cave women must have fashioned dolls of clay and grasses.

In archaeological sites from ancient Rome, Egypt, and China, excavators have found great numbers of crude toys. Ancient literature refers to toys in every language, and there were rag dolls and crude wooden rocking horses in every Pilgrim home where there were children.

Where and when the first commercial toys made their appearance is anybody's guess, but there is evidence that it all started in Holland. At one time, all of Europe was flooded with wonderful, ingenious toys from this country and others, mechanical wonders: dolls that danced and talked, clowns that did stunts, horses that galloped, donkeys that brayed and kicked, monkeys that chattered and climbed, cows that mooed and could be milked.

The early 1900s was the great toy era in this country. The cost of materials was very low. Many toys were made of heavy steel or iron or pewter. Tin was the least expensive of all, and gaily painted, clever tin toys could be bought for as little as 10 or 15 cents, heavy iron toys for 50 cents or a dollar.

I had three sisters and three brothers, and though we were not a wealthy family, we always received good toys at Christmastime. There were big, strong wagons, buses, trolley cars, engines, and trains. Any of these toys would bring a pretty penny today. Most of them are in museums.

I recall the kicking-mule bank that I saw in a store window when I was about ten years old. I coveted it. It was priced at $1.98, a lot of money to spend on a toy in those days, but I wanted it so badly. I agreed to ask for nothing more and I got it! I kept it for many years.

What happened to it I don't know, but I saw one exactly like it pictured in a toy catalog, and priced at $250. How strange that I, so young, would know that such a toy was a very worthwhile item. Insert a coin, and the black boy was kicked over by the mule. The words below read, "Oh! How I 'spise a mule," which would be frowned on today.

I recall a spinning doll that a favorite uncle of mine bought me one Christmas. It was made of steel and was mounted on a platform that was a music box. She was beautiful—dressed in blue fabric glistening with rhinestones. But the wonder of it all was, when you placed it on the back of the range, the gentle heat caused it to pirouette as the music played, revolving around and around. I've never seen anything like it. I'm quite sure it is a French toy. I still have it, but it was so loved and used, it does not work anymore.

I recall, too, a string pull toy I had when I was about eight years old. It was called "Simple Simon and the Goose." When the string was pulled the goose opened his beak, made a screeching sound, and grasped at Simon's pants. And Simon opened his mouth and howled. It was very funny and quite ingenious. The cost was 25 cents.

My brothers had fire engines that would be the envy of any small boy today. These engines and trucks were made of very heavy iron, and were finely detailed. They were equipped with movable ladders and hoses that really worked. There were galloping horses and firemen dressed in bright uniforms and steel helmets. If you could find such a toy today, it would be priced way up in the hundreds. They must have cost only a dollar or two at that time (about 1913).

I loved the little blue-and-white cow I received one Christmas, and I kept it for many years. It gave out a very lifelike "moo" and, if you put milk into it and pumped its tail up and down, it could be milked. I also had a wooden duck that quacked and wobbled along in a very realistic way.

I remember a windup toy, with a black drummer sitting on a barrel. His coat was a vivid yellow, his trousers a bright red, his hat bright green. Wind him up and he'd drum for an hour, loud and clear, and when he stopped, he'd tip his hat: a wonderful toy!

When cars first appeared on our city streets in the early 1900s, toy manufacturers began making them in miniatures. They cost from 50 cents to a dollar. One of the very first that I recall was a Hercules bus. It was heavy, black, and highly polished, and it was my brother's favorite toy. It had real rubber tires and the wheel really steered. The horn honked, and there was a driver dressed in a uniform.

At one time, we had a real trolley car, with passengers that could be moved around, a conductor with a money belt holding little coins, and a clanging bell for off and on. It was about a foot long. We enjoyed many an hour with that trolley car. Toys such as these are now historic items, and desirable collectibles, as are airplane miniatures of the pioneer age. My brothers had many of these early toy planes, clever and wonderfully made.

Of course boys love military toys and we had plenty of those. But they have not withstood the years; they were played with too long and too hard. The poor old toys—we had them all. Ives was a famous name, and so was American Flyer.

We had building and alphabet blocks that went through all the children, loved by each one and given over reluctantly to the next in line. The old Noah's Ark was in our toy box, too, with its many wooden animals in line. The ark itself was colorfully decorated and the animals had nodding heads, rolling eyes, and moving legs.

There were thousands of toy boats in the early 1900s. We had, at one time, a replica of Robert Fulton's first steamboat. The wooden paddle really revolved and the stack blew real smoke from a tiny pellet placed inside. And there was a tiny sailboat to be placed in a tub of water. It was not a windup toy. I cannot recall what it was that made it navigable, but it sailed around and around the tub, and whistled too.

I remember a sturdy milk truck we loved to play with. It held eight bright, tin milk cans with handles and covers, to fill and deliver over and over again. There were meat trucks with miniature hams and chickens, and baker's trucks with tiny loaves of bread; lumber trucks filled with tiny logs, and coal trucks that could dump a load of coal.

But the toys that interested me most were the curious little windup toys that were usually sold by vendors on the streets. These ingenious toys appeared just once and then were never seen for sale again. So, if found in good condition, they bring very high prices today. There were little tin jumping dogs, tumbling clowns, whirling clowns and dancing men, elephants that bowed and seals that could throw a ball . . . and many, many more.

These toys were picked up for 10 cents or a quarter, brought home to a child, played with until broken, then thrown away; that is why so few are to be found today. It's hard to believe that one of these toys in good condition could bring at least $100 today.

During World War I, when metal was a priority product, the production of toys almost ceased. And these curious little toys disappeared. After the war, the toy industry turned to plastic. The early plastics were very unsatisfactory, easily broken.

We have now entered the age of dolls that walk, talk, cry, and wet; animals to ride upon; cars that travel; space objects that fly — wonderful things! But the toys of my childhood will never fade from my memory.

Christmas Shopping with
Great-Aunt Amanda

GREAT-AUNT AMANDA WAS GRANDMA'S SISTER. WE never called her anything else but Aunt or Auntie Mandy. She came to visit us every year, just before Christmas. She lived in a very small town in Maine and she thought Worcester was a great metropolis. We loved her, but Aunt Mandy was more than a bit odd. Her voice was loud and harsh, with a nasal twang, and she was very deaf.

"I'm a leetle deaf," she would shout. "You'll have to speak up." She was nearsighted, too, and she wore her glasses halfway down her nose. She came by train, and when she disembarked, lugging a huge carpetbag, she beamed at us, and called us all by name.

"Jen, you've grown so, and Bea, my little bunny." She wore a voluminous cape, which came to her ankles, high-button shoes, long black gloves, and a felt hat with a red rose sticking up straight from it. Aunt Mandy was known as a dresser.

It was my turn to go shopping with her that year,

and I dreaded the task. It was very humiliating—she was loud in her ways—and I was a very quiet, rather shy little girl. I was about thirteen years old at the time I helped her unpack. She had Mother Hubbards for day wear, many petticoats trimmed with handmade tatting and lace, black alpaca dresses for Sunday wear, and many large, white aprons.

We loved the evenings when Auntie Mandy was with us, for she would tell us stories of her childhood and early life. She told us about the great blizzard of 1880 when the snow was so deep that they were shut in for days. Her old father got lost in the howling wind and snow and Auntie Mandy found him half a mile away from the house, nearly frozen to death. She herself dragged him back to the house and revived him, and he lived quite a few more years, until he was over a hundred.

She kept her savings in a Worcester bank, so "the furst thing off," she'd say, "is to go and make a drawin'."

Entering the bank, she peered around. "Oh, dear! This can't be the right bank. Where is my Mr. Slezac?" A clerk came up and asked, "What's the trouble, miss? Can I be of service to you?"

"Where is Mr. Slezac? He should be right in this corner. Oh, dear! Where is he? He's got my money. I must be in the wrong bank."

He assured her that it was the right bank. But it had been remodeled, and Mr. Slezac was not employed there any more.

"Oh, dear," she screamed. "Why didn't you leave it alone? And how am I going to get my money?"

The clerk was very gracious, and helped her to draw out the one hundred dollars she needed. She couldn't write, so I had to sign her name, under her cross, and she coached me every step of the way. "Right here, do it neat. Don't tell them what I want it for," etc., etc.

To me, a hundred dollars seemed like a fortune, and I was very worried about it. She stuffed it carelessly in her "reticule" and grabbed my arm. "Let's go, child." She thanked the clerk, and yelled "Goodbye" to all the others.

But, as we left the bank, she slipped and fell. Down she went, her hat over one eye, her skirts over her head, showing her white-lace-trimmed underdrawers. At first, she was as mad as could be, but after a bit, her sense of humor emerged. She laughed, and set herself upright, saying with a twinkle in her eye, "Might's well have a leetle rest." A few people had gathered, but she paid them no attention; she just straightened her clothes, and we proceeded into town.

Everywhere you looked, the city was beautiful. Lights twinkled like stars on poles. Boys were selling pine wreaths and evergreens with big red bows on them. The air was fragrant and sweet from the scent of them. Aunt Mandy was radiant. Everything amused her and stimulated her. "Oh, isn't this just loverly. Oh, Christmas is such a wonderful time!"

We went into a big department store always known

as "The Boston Store" (Denholm and McKay). In the dress department, a clerk came hurrying to us. "What can we do for you, madam?" she queried.

"I want to buy a princess dress," Aunt Mandy declared. Princess dresses were all the rage at that time, and Aunt Mandy had "set her heart" on one. "The purtiest one you have," she demanded. I knew it was hopeless, as she was shaped like a barrel, and that style was intended for slim people.

They brought out the largest size they had in stock. They tugged and they tugged, and finally got it on her. She looked into the full-length mirror. "I'm bumpier 'n a toad," she said, "and just as ugly." She looked like an umbrella in a very fat case. Then her common sense took over. "I guess a princess dress ain't for me."

They showed her other dresses but she liked none of them. "Ain't fitten to wash dishes in" was her comment. And her mood was changing. Then I got a bright idea. "Auntie Mandy, you sew so well. Why don't we buy some pretty dress goods and a pattern and make a dress to fit you well?"

"Now that's what I call thinking," she said. We walked over to the dress-goods department, and the clerk showed her bolt after bolt of material. Finally, my heart sank when she chose a hideous yellow and brown check. "Oh, Auntie, not that one," I protested. But nothing else would do. "Wrap it careful, now," she shouted. "I don't want it wrinkled." Then, after hearing the price, she declared, "Five dollars!

Why, that's highway robbery." But it was settled, and we walked out with the package in my arms.

Next, we went to a fine restaurant down in the basement. "I'm hungrier 'n a green toad," she said, as we found a table. Aunt Mandy thought everything delicious, and she insisted on talking with the chef, so they called him in.

"Those dumplin's were just puffick," she said, loud enough for everyone in the room to hear. "And your apple pie is as good as mine. It always wins a prize at the county fair, too. So, that's sayin' a lot for you." Then, she added, "I'll send you my recipe for my filled raisin cookies when I get back home." As we left, she waved to everyone. "Good-bye, and Merry Christmas." Her good mood had returned.

Next step was the Hat Emporium on Main Street. We were lucky there, for she fell in love with a hat in the window. It was a large-brimmed hat that had a bird with red feathers perched on the crown. I could visualize it with the yellow-and-brown-check dress. But I said nothing. I was getting very tired, and I told Aunt Mandy so.

"Why should a child like you get tired?" she scolded. "Now, we are going to get to the real Christmas shopping." She was just getting into full sail. We walked and we walked, and we bought and we bought: a bright flowered tie for conservative Uncle Fred; a sewing kit for Aunt Rose, who hated to sew; an apron for Aunt Lucy, who never did any housework; a red vest for Pa, who didn't own a suit.

We were bogged down with bundles. I was exhausted. "I want to go home," I said. Aunt Mandy peered at me in exasperation. But she consented to sit down a few moments on a bench on the common, while she proceeded to tie some of the packages together with a piece of string she took from her reticule.

"We got one more thing to buy then we'll go home," she said. "Now, for the surprise!" Then, "Did you notice that dress just about your size in the Boston Store window?" she asked. Oh, yes, I had noticed it. It was a dream of a dress. Flowered challis, with a sweet lace collar, and a dear little red belt. I forgot my tiredness. But I cried, "Oh, no! It would be too expensive."

"Oh, pshaw!" said Aunt Mandy. "It's your Christmas, too, you are a good girl, and I'm not going to bring any of this money back home. If it fits you, I'll buy it."

Oh, it had to fit! And it did.

Aunt Mandy beamed. "Oh. That's the purtiest thing on you." And as they wrapped it up, she admonished them. "Don't you dare get a wrinkle in it. Lawsy me! Are you goin' to look purty on Christmas Day." I was so happy I was trembling. Never had I dreamed that the day would turn out like this.

As we boarded the trolley car on our way home, Aunt Mandy greeted everyone. "Merry Christmas, everybody." Her mood was contagious. Even the conductor smiled at her and answered her, "Merry

Christmas to you, too." A little boy gave her a sprig of evergreen for her coat. Everyone in the trolley car was waving and smiling as we got off, and calling "Merry Christmas to all."

Dear Aunt Mandy. What if she was a little odd? Her heart was pure gold. And I loved her.

When the Drummers
Came to Town

WHEN I WAS A CHILD, OUR HOME WAS NEAR MAIN
Street, Worcester, and the few inns and taverns of the
town were not very far away. Fear was not instilled in
children in those days, and we were free to walk the
length of Main Street and make friends where we
wished to. The drummers who came to town were
my friends. Grandpa had a shoe shop, and he knew
many of them.

From earliest times, men have drifted in and out of
towns taking up the occupation of traders—traveling
salesmen, knights of the road, peddlers, drummers.
How well I remember them! They brought wonder
and excitement into my life. When they left, the days
grew dull.

When a man stepped out of an omnibus a hundred
years ago onto the Main Street of almost any New
England town, he would hear the heavy clop-clop of
horses' hoofs. The shrill cries of many vendors trying

to sell their wares filled the air, but drummers were in a different category.

They carried heavy cases of sample goods (called drums), or, if the line was a large item, they carried miniatures of the real thing. Sometimes, when a drummer had received a new sample, he would leave the old miniature to a favorite child on his route—a tiny wringer, a little mattress for a doll's bed, a little broom, or a tiny sadiron (a kind of flatiron). When I was given a tiny wooden icebox, I wept for joy.

The drummer we watched for most eagerly was the watch man, with the fabulous watches and tricky charms he displayed in the foyer of Mechanic's Hall. He would give away little replicas with hands that really moved and stems that really wound up. We loved the trade cards he gave too, of "the watch that never stops." There were always riddles and puzzles on them.

In those early days, the drummer was a glamorous figure in the eyes of his fellow men. He was a man of great sophistication. He traveled extensively at a time when few men strayed from their own domain. He was in touch with the outside world. He attended the big fairs and expositions. He could order from a bill of fare with flair. And hadn't he seen with his own eyes Eva Tanguay, Harry Lauder, and Sarah Bernhardt? He'd even seen something called moving pictures, pictures come to life.

Often he was an entertainer as well as a salesman. He might be a ventriloquist, or a fiddler, or a singer.

He would visit the old country store where the old men were sitting around the potbellied stove, and thrill them with his charms and talent. One could draw pennies from Grandpa's ears; another could sing "Listen to the Mockingbird," and whistle to make the birds envious.

My grandfather was a shoemaker and a good one. He bought his leathers and findings from a drummer named Roland. Roland once gave me tiny leather shoes for my doll. He always smelled strongly of leather, and his sample case held many, many strips of gleaming, soft, supple leathers of all shades, which I loved to touch.

It was from my grandfather's shop in Main Street that I watched the calliope go by. The drummers loved the calliope, a steam piano invented by a man named Stoddard, and they would often get up a little impromptu parade.

The calliope made its debut on the streets of Worcester in July 1895 and was an instant hit. Every circus that came to town used the calliope, but the drummers could never wait for a circus; they had to get the calliope out. Grandpa said that was because they had a part in putting it together, but I couldn't vouch for that.

Though a few knew all the cozy corners in town, and knew the "ladies of light virtue" who had not been rounded up by the Magdalen Female Benevolent Society, the majority of them were good family men. Sample cases were heavy, it was strenuous work, and they needed a good night's sleep. Many nights a drummer had to sleep in a cold depot, waiting for his train to take him to his next destination. It was not an easy life.

In even earlier days (the late 1700s) he was a carrier of news and letters from one customer to another, and he was eagerly awaited. Father used to tell me that, before my time, drummers were often asked to help out in time of need. At funerals, for instance, a drummer would often be asked to help the local merchant (who had himself been a drummer) dress the body and serve as pallbearer or even help dig the grave, for often there was no undertaker in town.

In the town hall of Lenox there is a document addressed to a merchant: "Richard Hale has lost his good wife. If you will let him have the necessary articles for the funeral, the town will exchange them for such items as you will select from a drummer's supply—but let prudence, economy and generosity mark your selection, please. Also, please some crepe for his hat. P.S. Maybe the drummer would kindly serve as pallbearer."

I have seen this ad in an old ledger, dated 1890: "This account not collectible. He ran off somewheres. Just a no-good, dead-beat drummer, who I bought things from, and he got his hair cut, too. He owes me board and room for two weeks—that #!&*$!#&*!"

In a *Hartford Courant* from 1861, a merchant advertised for 1,500 hanks of rope and, of all things, 10 three-year-old mules, in exchange for "things a drummer would like."

Another Connecticut paper, the *Middletown Gazette*, wanted spices, indigo, slates, liniments, tools, medicines, calico, soaps, tea, sponges, and ladies' bonnets: "Would welcome a 'small-goods' drummer here."

In a *Boston Gazette* from 1830: "Will exchange chickens for tobacco, maple sugar, candles, frying pans, heavy stockings."

In some biographical notes, I read that Paul Revere was once a drummer during hard times, from 1779 to 1792. People were buying pottery rather than silver. He sold many things: spectacles, false teeth, wallpaper, toupees, pumice stones, and, of course, "silver plate, in the newest taste, and neatest manner."

The story goes that it was a drummer who first asked for a Bible in his hotel room, and the Gideon International, inspired by the request, placed thousands of Bibles in rooms, and are still doing it. Most of the drummers who came to town attended church on Sundays, and joined in the singing with enthusiasm. If someone invited them to a Sunday dinner, for chicken pie and dumplings, it was accepted with great delight.

One incident I recall vividly was at a gala event in Worcester in 1902. A visiting drummer broadcast that he intended to scale the highest steeple in town, on City Hall. A crowd gathered. He not only kept his word, but did some balancing acts at the top, causing the crowd to scream and tremble with fear. That was the most excitement Worcester had had for many a day.

Worcester was a favorite stopping place for drummers. There was always a good brisk trade, and it was considered quite a lovely place. The Old Bay State Hotel on Main Street was a favorite. Before that it had been the Heywood tavern, operated by generations of Heywoods. I'll always remember the plush parlor which, to me, seemed the very highest attainment of elegance. And I was fascinated by the shooting equipment displayed in the lobby.

At the corner of Main and Elm streets was another very popular tavern with the drummers. Called the King's Arms, it was built in 1732 by Thomas Stevens, and run by him for over fifty-two years. It was a meeting place for Tories during the Revolution. Afterwards it became the Lincoln House. In 1875 it was the Worcester House, and it was there for a great many years. It was before my time, of course, but I heard a great deal about it.

The Exchange Hotel at the corner of Main and Market streets was the largest and most pretentious hotel, and only the more successful of the drummers could afford to stay there. Some of them were the Graham salesmen. The Graham era made a lot of money for many people. There were Graham hotels and Graham boardinghouses where only Graham products were served. The fever had swept the country like fire.

The founder of the Graham phenomenon was Sylvester Graham, a lecturer and reformer, formerly a drummer, who preached "The Science of Life." He was against tobacco, bleached flour, meat, and hard liquor. He claimed Graham products would bring health to all. Butchers hated him and he was once attacked by a mob in Boston. But he made some drummers rich.

When paper products came in, that was also a heyday for the drummers. In the early 1800s, Dexter and Sons introduced paper packages on a wire loop to hang in the bathroom or outhouse. Before that, catalogs and newspapers served the purpose. The first drummer to bring in the new rolls couldn't get rid of them. It took a long while for them to catch on.

The earlier drummers (and peddlers and hawkers) had a much harder time than the later ones did, in every way. Traveling was very slow. It took a complete day to go from Worcester to Boston by coach in the early 1700s. And the coach could accommodate only twelve passengers, tightly seated. The coach would set off from the tavern in the darkness of morning, as the clock chimed five o'clock, and it would be the dark of evening before it would reach Boston, stopping at the Lion's Tavern in Marlborough for lunch.

The *Massachusetts Spy*, printed by Isaiah Thomas, carried an ad that stated, "The firm of Pease and Sykes will carry drummers from Hartford to Worcester with 14 pounds of luggage, for 3 pence a mile, in good weather. Also will provide decent lodging for them." This gives us proof that they were in good standing in that early day.

But in 1750, a law went into effect that "pedlars, hawkers, and drummers may not solicit goods in public places." A fine of twenty shillings was enforced, "half of which shall go to the poor." The drummers and peddlers had to take to the country, which was a real hardship.

The law was repealed in 1789. In 1850, industry was thriving, and all sorts of goods were badly needed. In Taunton, more than two hundred industries were reported: stoves, silverware, and copper (Rolly Industries, later Revere Ware) were the main ones.

Dighton, Somerset, and Swansea were all fine stops for drummers before they went to Newport, which was fast becoming a wealthy seaport town. Lamps were becoming a very important sales item at this time, about 1850, when lighting was undergoing a great change. The Argand burner, which came in many decorative styles and colors, was a big seller that made some drummers rich.

Many now famous men were peddlers, the forerunners of drummers: Benjamin Altman, Adam Gimbel, Marshall Field, and Meyer Guggenheim, the founder of the great copper industry. There are many others. It is said that the famous Levi's were named for the famous Levi Strauss, who got his start by selling shoestrings on the street for five cents each, and who started out with one single dime for capital.

From wayfarers who traveled over dusty roads on foot, then on horseback, then by horse and wagon, then to the swift transportation of railroad, then finally by automobile, the way now takes to the skies.

In the late 1700s a new set of conditions came into existence. Steam navigation made it possible for drummers to visit out-of-the-way places never before attempted. By the late 1800s steamboats were big business indeed, and in the early 1900s they were luxurious. Drummers could, and did, travel in great style.

Today's drummers, salesmen, are a very different breed from the old days. They conduct business in a glamorous restaurant over a hearty meal and a beverage. Perhaps they might meet in an airport. A big deal with thousands of dollars involved might be wrapped up in an hour or so. Papers signed . . . a handshake . . . and it's over. Men are still drawn to the game of barter and sale, but the old charm is gone.

Mother's Infatuation
with Honest Abe

So was it when my life began;
So is it now I am a man;
So be it when I shall grow old . . .

THAT LITTLE VERSE BY WORDSWORTH WAS OFTEN quoted by Abraham Lincoln. It reminds us that everything that has a bearing on your life as a child will influence your life as an adult. The stories you hear, the pictures on the wall, the books on the shelves, all will contribute to your character and cast the mold of what kind of a man or woman you will be.

My mother was five months old when Lincoln was shot down. All during her childhood she heard stories of Lincoln: his early life, his achievements, and his assassination. It impressed her greatly. Lincoln was her hero. "The greatest man that ever lived," she would say, "and the most abused president of all time."

All during her lifetime she collected a great many clippings from newspapers and magazines, and she would read these to us children. "His greatness was not realized," she would tell us, "until after his death in 1865." Often he was pictured as a scarecrow, and described as a grotesque, awkward, ugly character. He was often called an ape, and "bag o' bones," and many other horrid names. Many cartoons pictured him covering his face with his cloak.

All these things raised my mother's ire, as soon as she was old enough to sense their meaning. And she always resented the fact that people made more of Washington's birthday than they did of Lincoln's. She read everything she could find about his assassination and never got over the horror of it. President Roosevelt's famous phrase about the bombing of Pearl Harbor was probably coined by my mother: "A date which will live in infamy."

She owned and prized a book, a sort of history of Worcester which told stories of Abe Lincoln (I never heard her call him anything but Abe) and the lives of other Lincolns in Worcester. Levi Lincoln was the first mayor of Worcester, and a well-known lawyer. He was the one who invited Abe Lincoln to come to Worcester in 1848 when he was making a tour of New England, and the future president accepted.

During the meeting, when Levi introduced him to the audience, the two Lincolns tried to trace their ancestry. Abe delighted them all when he said, "I hope I belong to your clan, as the Scotch say, but if we are both good Whigs, who cares?"

Today, we know more about Lincoln's ancestry than he ever knew. His direct ancestor, authorities believe, was Samuel Lincoln, who came from England to Hingham in 1637 at the age of seventeen.

In our home, there was a fine framed picture of Lincoln, taken at the time of his Worcester visit, and I never thought of him as anything but handsome. The title beneath his picture read "Honest Abe," but he was not always called that. It is said that it was in New England that he acquired that title, as New Englanders liked this tall, awkward rail-splitter from Illinois.

Many New England journals praised him highly as "The Pride of Illinois," and in New Hampshire the *Independent Democrat* called him "masterly" and "convincing." The *Providence Journal* also lauded him: "He abounds in good humor, and gives a thrust as sharp as a Damascus blade."

The Worcester book held many of these clippings and pictures, and a long account of the Worcester visit: "The cheers could be heard for miles around as he was escorted through the streets to City Hall. After greeting the crowd, he said that he felt very small and modest here among wise and educated people. He said that the free soil party reminded him of the peddler who offered a pair of pants for sale, 'too small for a man, but too big for a boy.'"

He said it made him very sad to travel through a certain town and see many mills manned by small boys and girls, children who should have been out in the sunshine. "I have heard that there are eight thousand children working in one city alone," he said, "and I am certainly going to do something about that if I get the chance." And he did.

One story told of a wag in the audience who called out to Abe, "Did they kick you out of Illinois?" Two policemen started to eject the heckler from the hall, but Lincoln said, "No! Let him stay. I think he's got a darned good question there, and I want to answer him." The result was that a near riot turned to laughter. Even his critic applauded, and sat quietly to listen.

There was another incident that caused quite a fracas. At some statement that Lincoln made, two men jumped up and started to argue with him; others started to shout, "Put them out." Soon the whole crowd was in an uproar.

Lincoln shouted, "Let them be. . . . Let them talk. . . . I need someone to jaw at me, and I will listen if they let me talk back." They talked, and he answered, and he won his point. The audience was impressed.

By the time Lincoln had boarded his train back to Illinois, estimation of him had climbed to a new high. He was nominated on the Republican ticket in 1860 at the national convention in Chicago. New Englanders' responses varied, but most were enthusiastic. Some states fired one hundred salutes from one hundred guns. There were giant celebrations. But there were a few adverse reactions.

The state of Maine announced in one of its publications that "the nomination of Lincoln was followed by a very severe frost, and that was only natural." An item in the *Boston Courier,* which caused much street fighting, claimed that "the country has lost its senses." The *New Hampshire Patriot* observed that the gun salutes were "very feeble, the calibre of the guns being equal to the candidate."

The majority of the people said that "Old Abe" didn't stand a ghost of a chance. One Boston paper said, "The clodhopper will fade out quickly." A Worcester paper proclaimed that "if that clod, Lincoln, ever got to be president, he'd track mud through the rooms, and keep pigs on the lawn. He'd pile logs in the parlor, and serve corn-pone to his guests." Soon afterwards, this same paper was eating crow, praising his efforts.

In early November, the battle of words ended, and the battle to win the election was on. Mother told us the story many times (no doubt taken from this same book) of how, here in Worcester, a one hundred-year-old man by the name of Ebeneezer Mower walked five miles to the polling place to vote for Lincoln. He had voted for George Washington in 1789, and he wanted it to be known that he had retained his mental faculties by voting for Abe Lincoln, "Honest Abe."

In Maine, there was another centenarian, said to be

the sole survivor of Bunker Hill, named Ralph Farnum. He had to walk seven miles to the polls, and when he arrived he fired a shot from a pistol saying, "That's one more shot for independence." The story goes on that he made a little speech, and changed the minds of a few people. "Lincoln did not merely win in New England . . . he swept it clean." That was Mother's statement; she glowed as she said it.

When the dispatch of Lincoln's death was received, on April 14, 1865, it was nearly midnight. There was a great ringing of bells, and all the city was aroused. Many citizens rose from their beds and went out into the streets. Neighbors met and mourned. Nothing was accomplished the next day. It was as though the city itself had died.

The city council met at 7 A.M., and a public meeting was called to take place in Mechanic's Hall at 10 A.M. The Honorable Alexander Bullock presided, and the account said that it was a "most solemn and sad occasion." On April 23, 1865, there was a memorial given by the Reverend Seth Sweetzer which, the book says, "was attended by huge throngs, many of them weeping."

Another meeting was held in Mechanic's Hall soon after and a *Eulogy on Abe Lincoln,* written by Alexander Bullock, was delivered. The general public and all the city officials were invited. This eulogy was printed, and was sold at this meeting. I know Mother had one, but what became of it I do not know. I'm sure there are people who still have it, and treasure it.

Lincoln's birthday means more to me than it does to most people. But all Worcesterites, and indeed all New England, should be proud of the part our ancestors played in the life and election of Lincoln. He will never be forgotten. The deeds and the character of this man will live forever.

Winter Days in
the Early 1900s

IN SOME RESPECTS, WINTER WAS THE MOST DELIGHTFUL
season in the early 1900s. The hectic holidays were
over, school was closed till mid-January, and there
was time now to reap the harvest of summer, to enjoy
all the good things canned and bottled from the garden, and the leftovers from the Christmas baking.

And it was visiting time. There were very few
phones, so we got no warning of company about to
call. It was not unusual for a whole family to drop in
and announce their intention to stay overnight. For-
tunately, our house was large, with plenty of food and
plenty of room. Four kids might have to sleep in one
bed, but that was fun.

It was a time of parties too, all kinds of parties.
Taffy pulls were very popular. A big kettle of ingredients was put on the stove to boil, and we played
guessing games while it cooked. Then it was poured
on a slab to cool and we all took turns pulling and

twisting it until it was smooth and white. I lost the recipe long ago, but I know it was tart-sweet and delicious, melting on the tongue.

There were musical parties, where everyone stood around the piano and sang popular songs and hymns. And parties where the whole evening was spent playing games—rook, dominoes, old maid, guessing games, and charades. There didn't seem to be any "generation gap." Everyone participated, young ones, grownups, parents, grandparents, all ages and sexes. It would be a very poor family indeed that did not have a big party sometime during the winter. There was a togetherness that is not seen today.

And when there was snow on the ground (and it seemed there was, most of the time), there were the sled and toboggan parties. We used long, homemade toboggans that held five or six people. Most of the hilly streets of Worcester were safe to slide on, and there was very little traffic at night. Laughing and shouting, we'd go rapidly down the hill, right into the road, then climb right back up the hill. With red cheeks and bright eyes, it seemed we never felt the cold, not even on a zero-degree night.

Everyone loved the nights when we played charades, and we planned way ahead of time just what we should do. There was some very clever acting. Our method was for each player to act out a famous character—George Washington or Christopher Columbus or Saint Peter. Those who couldn't guess paid a forfeit. It was great fun.

I recall one evening of charades, when our neighbor Mr. Higgins, a very dignified man, was supposed to represent the devil. He lay flat on the floor and used his fingers for horns, with a most frightful leer on his face. No dignity whatsoever. We were never surprised at these people who did such unpredictable things. Everyone just broke down and had fun.

Those winter months were ideal for reading also. All our family were readers. There was a tall, wide bookcase in the upstairs hall that held all our favorites, including a complete set of Dickens. How I loved *The Old Curiosity Shop*, and read it again and again. There were many warm, cozy spots for reading in our big house, and fortified with apples and popcorn, I spent many happy winter hours in one of them, curled up with a book. No wonder I was a plump little girl.

We walked to the public library for more books. Children today would not be familiar with the titles of those books—*Wide, Wide World* and the Rollo books, *Our Foreign Cousins, Little Princess*, and others. I had read *Pride and Prejudice* when I was ten years old, though the librarian thought I was far too young for it. Too young indeed! I read anything I could lay my hands on.

My brothers had all the Horatio Alger books, and I read those too, and was very much impressed with the morals they conveyed. They should be republished.

It was the custom during this early winter vacation to visit with cousins for a few days. I so clearly remember the time I visited Uncle Nelson and Aunt

Mary in Woonsocket, Rhode Island. They had a very large family — six girls and five boys — and a very large house to accommodate them all. The dining room was enormous, furnished only with a long, long table with benches on either side. The whole family could be seated at that table, and still have room for five or six more.

Aunt Mary was stocky and jolly. She had trained each child to look after the next oldest, and she took care of the baby. They all helped with the housework, too. So Aunt Mary enjoyed her family, and she never looked tired or worn out. She was always up for a joke and loved to play a prank on her family.

On this particular day, I was seated with the family at the table. Aunt Mary always counted the children before we were served. She pretended that she never remembered how many she had. She counted, one, two, three, four. Then she came to me.

"Who is this one?" she shouted. "How did she get in here? Out; Out!" She yelled at me, "Go home, where you belong!" I was a very sensitive child, and I was terrified. I started to sob, and jumped from my seat. Aunt Mary was so remorseful. "Can't you take a joke, child?" She hugged me and kissed me, and all during the meal gave me extra helpings, and the biggest piece of pie. But I never forgot this episode, and always felt a little in awe of Aunt Mary.

Once my family was part of a clan, with relatives all over, in little suburban towns around Worcester. We could visit easily by trolley car or horse and buggy.

Everything seemed quiet and peaceful everywhere. Once in a while we heard a fire alarm or the "Black Maria" (ambulance) going by, but not often. A street fight once in a while. That was about it.

Now, we are scattered all over the country, and even with cars and planes, visits are few and far between. But there is a quiet place, very quiet, where each of the departed ones is remembered with plaque or slab bearing the name and dates of birth and death. To spend a little time there brings back a time of happy days in a different sort of world. In many ways it is a better world now, but I would love to see some of the old customs brought back.

The Thanksgiving That
Almost Wasn't

THE DAY THAT MAMA TURNED OVER THE OCTOBER PAGE in the big 1904 calendar that hung over the kitchen table, we knew that Thanksgiving would soon be here. For there was a picture of a family seated around a big table, on which was a platter holding a golden brown turkey, and dishes of steaming vegetables. That picture made my mouth water.

But I felt that this year, things would be different. Business was bad. Papa had been working only a few days a week. I doubted that we would have any golden brown turkey on our table this year. One of my uncles, Uncle Jim, sometimes raised a few turkeys, and sometimes gave us one, in exchange for a few of Mama's delicious apple pies. But this year, some ailment had hit the turkeys, and they were not doing well. He doubted that he would break even on them, if he was able to sell them at all.

We made a few preparations for the big day, but

Mama said that for once we might go without meat.
Perhaps we would have a stuffed haddock, or something like that. Fish was cheap and plentiful. I didn't
like fish much, and I wasn't looking forward to
Thanksgiving.

I didn't think I had much to be thankful for. But
Mama said, "If you think you don't have anything to
be thankful for, then be thankful for something you
don't have." "What, for instance?" I asked her.
"Well," she said, "You don't have whooping cough,
do you? You don't have measles; you don't have a
cold. Be thankful for all that."

One day, about two weeks before Thanksgiving,
Uncle Jim's big wagon came rumbling into our yard.
He jumped down from his high seat and took a big
crate from the rear of the wagon. There was a terrible
squawking, and when he opened the crate, a turkey
flew out. Uncle Jim wrestled with the big bird to get
him within the yard gate.

"I've brought you something—your Thanksgiving
dinner. You'll have to fatten him up quick—he's kinda
poorly." He surely was! He had a long scrawny neck,
big pale eyes, big bony feet as skinny as toothpicks,
and a red tassel hanging from his beak like a wet
bandage. No wonder Uncle Jim gave him to us. Who
would buy him?

I held out my hand to him, but he let out such a
squawk that I jumped back. Uncle Jim tied him to a
tree stump. "You'd better keep him tied," he said.
"He's pretty ornery, he might bite." Then he gave us a

bag of feed, jumped up in the wagon again, and said, "I must be on my way. He's all yours, little Jen."

"Well," I said, "We've got a turkey. Now, we must give him a name." Mama said, "You don't name turkeys, you just feed them." But I said, "We've got to call him something. Let's call him Felix. That's a good name for a turkey." So Mama said, "OK, he's yours now, to feed and look after."

That evening I filled a can with fresh water, and put his feed in a cracked bowl. I fed Felix and talked to him. He gobbled up everything, and then, to my amazement, he blinked his eyes at me and walked close to me. I stroked him. The second day I untied him and he followed me around the yard. Just gobble, gobble, gobble, no squawks. He didn't like to be tied, so I let him walk around the yard all day. He seemed very content, and he looked a little better.

The third morning I went down to breakfast and got a surprise. There was Felix looking in the window. Someone had left an apple crate under the window, and he had climbed up on it. When I came into the room he became excited, and let out a squawk. But it was not a bad noise, just a soft squawk. He waited there until I went out to feed him. Then he followed me around like Mary's little lamb. In less than a week, Felix had gained four pounds, and he surely was a better-looking turkey.

That evening we had gingerbread for dessert at supper. I had half of my piece and ran out to share it with Felix. He loved it. He gobbled it down and looked for more. After that, I always shared my dessert with him. He loved corn muffins, apple pie, tapioca pudding, and any kind of cookies. I think Mama suspected I was sharing my dessert, for she started giving me larger pieces. Felix just loved everything Mama cooked. No wonder he was looking better.

About three days before Thanksgiving, I saw Mama looking at Felix. Then she looked at Papa. "When are you going to kill him?" she asked. I jumped up from my chair. "You are not going to kill Felix!" I screamed. "Uncle Jim gave him to me. He's mine!" To my surprise, my brother sided with me. "Ah, Ma! Felix is her pet. We don't have to have turkey every year."

"Well," said Mama. "This calls for a conference. Maybe we'll just forget about Thanksgiving this year. We'll just have an ordinary dinner." "That's fine with me," I said. "I love fish anyway."

Mama looked at me with her lips pressed tightly. "I'll remember that. You've never liked it before." No more was said, and I walked away, Felix following me.

That evening, another uncle dropped in. He was my youngest uncle, Uncle Joe, and I loved him dearly. After hugging us all, he said to Mama, "I hope you'll invite me to dinner Thanksgiving. And I hope you are going to have one of your wonderful chicken pies. I got a bonus this year, and I want to pay for the chicken." He took some bills from his pocket and gave them to Mama.

Of course, she argued a little, but he insisted. "I'm looking forward to it," he said. "No one makes chicken pie like yours. I can taste it already." So, it was settled.

I'm sure that somehow Uncle Joe had heard the story of Felix, and since he loved me, had decided to settle the thing for himself. It was a wonderful solution. We had a beautiful and delicious dinner. Felix stood on his crate under the window and watched us while we ate, making soft little squawks and gobbles.

I can't remember what became of Felix. But this I do know. We never ate him!

Clothes of Another Day

FASHIONS TODAY ARE SO SIMPLE, SO UNCLUTTERED, compared to the fashions in my youth. When I was young, clothes were a major part of my misery. They caused rows, naughtiness, unpleasantness — I hated to be dressed up. How I would have loved the shorts and T-shirts that the kids wear today.

Mother took a great deal of pains with our clothes. She spent hours and hours cutting up old dresses, and putting them back together again in all sorts of combinations and with added embellishments — flounces, laces, inserts, ruffles. My sister always seemed to look attractive in these homemade creations, but I always felt like a frump in mine.

My share of this business of dressmaking was picking out stitches, and Lord, how I hated it. When there was just too much of it, I really made a scene. I hated to put down my favorite fairy tales, or the latest issue of *St. Nicholas,* a monthly for children that I loved. Mother used to say I was the quietest of her children, but also the most provoking.

I spurned my mother's best efforts. I hated my clothes, and thought they made me look horrible. I detested the long, fleece-lined drawers I had to wear in cold weather. They bunched up at the knees, and twisted around my heavy lisle stockings. I hated the "ferris" waists that pinched my waist painfully and gaped loosely at the top where, as yet, there was nothing to fill it in. (Later on, that situation was reversed.)

I hated the leg-of-mutton sleeves, which were popular for so long. These gave me the feeling I was stuffed for the oven. I hated the big hats, heavy with yards and yards of ribbon. They had to be tied under the chin with elastic, which left red marks and pushed your ears forward.

I recall one such hat, a special purchase for my birthday. A leghorn straw, with seventeen yards of wide green satin ribbon. Mother said it made me look "so picturesque." It cost the whole of a five-dollar bill—a tremendous expense in those days. That amount would feed a family a whole week. But I was really happy when that hat went sailing over the lake one day, when I had forgotten to tie the elastic under my chin. Perhaps.

Anyway, from the "ferris" waist hung two long, black garters to hold up my stockings, which they seldom did. They were always becoming unbuckled, and my stockings falling down to trip me. Or, if they were not fastened tight enough, my stockings would lie in ugly wrinkles around my fat legs. Or if fastened too tight, they would strain on my shoulders, or make raw blisters on my thighs. The loose stockings would often bulge over my high-laced, black patent-leather shoes, making my legs look like sausages—big, fat ones.

And hair! In those days it was something one worked on continually. It was frizzed, curled, burnt, put up on rag, combed over "rats"—a sort of matted roll which made a pompadour. (That, by the way, was named for Madame Pompadour, mistress of Louis XV, who always wore her hair in that ridiculous fashion.)

Young girls usually did their hair up at night in strips of cloth to make corkscrew curls. I would never submit to this torture. Besides, I did have a little natural curl in my hair, so I tied it back with a ribbon in winter; and in summer, I took the shears and clipped it close to my head, in the privacy of my room, even though I knew it meant punishment.

Older girls had curling irons, which they put into the gas flame of an open burner. With this hot iron, they made frizzy bangs over their foreheads, and coy curls over their ears. The odor of burning hair often pervaded a room. It was not unusual for a child to lay her head upon an ironing board and have her tresses heated and curled with a flatiron.

To get back to the clothes: My dresses were usually made of cotton, and Mother starched them heavily, making them all the more uncomfortable. She also starched my petticoats, which were trimmed with stiff lace, or "hamburg," an embroidered cotton material. In summer, I wore cotton drawers, slit up the back and also trimmed with lace of hamburg. Often these drawers were a bit longer than my dress and showed beneath it, no matter how I pulled and tugged at them. I was forever embarrassed by them.

Once a year, at Easter time, my mother had a local dressmaker come in to help her make our dresses for the day. Everyone attended church on Easter morning with brand-new clothes on. It was torture to stand for an hour on a chair, to be turned and pushed and pinned. I was the worst one, the dressmaker told my mother, "the wiggliest young 'un I ever saw." I must have been, as my dresses never turned out right—hems always uneven, sleeves crooked, stripes askew.

I simply made up my mind that I could never be well dressed as my mother and sister were. Or good looking, or graceful, or charming. Fancy clothes were wasted on me, I thought, and only made me feel ridiculous and self-conscious. So I rebelled. And let them know that, from then on, I would wear only the clothes of my own choosing, or none at all. I sought the very simplest of patterns and learned to make my own clothes. I was free.

When I was eighteen, I wore plain wide skirts and plain white shirtwaists. But my skirts were long, and came way down to the ground. The fashion was to gather one side of the skirt into one hand, pulling it up with a graceful flair. But I seldom thought to do this, so each night I would have to brush the dried mud from my skirt. They were never washed, just brushed and aired.

The shirtwaists had to be boiled and starched and ironed. When I see the lovely blouses in the shops today that can be popped in the washer, hung up to dry, then worn without a wrinkle, I get angry all over again because of the clothes of my youth. It is quite a fad now to pick up these old-fashioned garments in antique shops, and they bring a good price. So look to see if there are any in your old aunt's attic. And pity the wearers.

I Remember Cupboards

Confused and dismayed by the hassles of today, many a human heart retreats into yesterday. Memory throws a glamor over the past, softening its harsh notes, and omitting its pitfalls.

It always amazes me when I hear people say, as many do, that they can remember nothing of their own childhood. I may forget a doctor's appointment, or to return a book to the library, but forget my childhood? I have only to press the mental key that recalls the year and the incident I want to think about.

I think we always remember best those things, customs, and traditions that are close to the heart. And so I often wonder—what has happened to cupboards? In the big old Victorian houses I used to visit as a child, there were cupboards in every room. Today, we have cabinets in the kitchen, but the cupboards in the other rooms are missing. In my childhood memories, cupboards come into focus sharply, fascinating and delightful to recall.

The cupboards in these houses were not after-thoughts added haphazardly. They were built in purposefully, planned as an integral part of the house, and as much a part of a day's living as the stove or the fireplace. And I firmly believe they had an effect on the growth and character of the children who lived with them.

The housewife took her cupboards seriously. It was her "bounden" duty to keep them locked, and to know each key as she knew her cooking utensils. To forget which was which would indicate a mind utterly frivolous. These keys were with her always.

The cupboards varied greatly in size and shape, each spelling its own peculiar charm to the child who was allowed to view the treasure kept there—but only occasionally. One never knew when or where one might come upon them, or what they might contain. There were tall and narrow ones beside the fireplace and short and stubby ones up above them. They were hidden behind the wainscoting, deeply secretive, or frankly and openly beside a window. Some could be reached only by a ladder. Many were the children, now perhaps gone from the scene, who were thrilled by the opening of those doors.

In one house I remember there was a cupboard that pretended to be part of a stenciled wall, but was in reality a storage space for guns. In another, there was a long, narrow cupboard about which hung a terrible legend of a child having smothered to death there within its walls, while playing a game of hide-and-seek. I always hurried past this place.

Foremost in my memory of delightful cupboards is the one which took up a high corner in a sunny dining room in Aunt Mary's house. Aunt Mary was a kindly soul, stout and good-natured, who always had a stray or two among her large brood of children. If a child was hurt in any way, she had a quick remedy for relieving the pain. "Let's see what Aunt Mary can find in the cupboard for you," she was wont to say. Out would come an array of delightful objects: tiny pieces of doll furniture, little carved animals, small jointed dolls, colorful glass beads, spinning tops, and many other rare and wonderful things. It was difficult to make a choice. Aunt Mary needed no psychologist to solve her children's problems. The cupboard was all it took.

Another cupboard that comes easily to mind is the cupboard over the fireplace in Great-Aunt Sarah's house in New Bedford. A most tantalizing odor came from this cupboard when it was opened. A hint of the spiciness of rich, dark cake, a provocative aroma of candied ginger, a certain affable sweetness, yet with a touch of sourness, difficult to describe, but mouth-watering even now as I recall it. It must have emanated from the very walls of the cupboard, so long had her delicacies been locked there within. The wonderful things in Great-Aunt Sarah's cupboard were not doled out to children. They were either too rich or too precious. There were squat round-shouldered jars with foreign-looking labels, tins of English biscuits, slender blue jars enclosed in bamboo containing sweetmeats. Square tins with delightful colored pictures on them full of soft squares called "Turkish Delight." Little tanks of tamarinds, and glass jars of rock candy. The rock candy we could have, and the tamarinds, she would say, were "good for little tummies." If we complained of a stomachache, she would make us a glass of tamarind water to drink down. The tamarind made the water sort of blackish, and it tasted a little of ginger.

In Great-Grandfather's house the cupboard in the parlor was deep and wide, and held a dozen or more bottles of liquor. When the pastor came to call, he was very tired and in need of nourishment, for churches were far and wide apart, and he traveled long distances. The cupboard was opened then. One bottle was labeled "Madeira Rum," and other "Finest Brandy." And there were many bottles of Great-Grandmother's homemade wines. Great-Grandmother wore the key around her neck, and even Great-Grandfather had to have permission to open it.

The candy cupboard in a house where a schoolmate of mine lived was a great favorite; when those doors were opened, I almost swooned with delight. Here were fat jars with ground-glass stoppers, filled with peppermint sticks, licorice sticks, blackjack balls, Gibraltars, molasses taffy, cinnamon drops, coconut squares, and many other delights to satisfy every craving for sweetness and stickiness.

One home I visited with my mother had a deep and wide cupboard built in the dining room. It was filled with precious china, much of it brought from over the sea via the China trade route. There was a set of the first old willow ware with the bridge and the two doves flying above—the legend being that of the lovers, fleeing from the angry parents, having been turned into doves by a kind protector. There were pieces of dainty Lowestoft, and on the topmost shelf, silver and copper luster pitchers. There was a lovely flowered tureen with a finial of a deep red rose. And in another smaller cupboard, a set of pure white dishes with a golden band on every piece. It was called "wedding-band" china. Even at that time, it was considered very precious, and used only for important company. The cups were as fragile as eggshells.

One kitchen cupboard that I recall held a great many pieces of old blue Staffordshire pottery china, which was then called "poor man's china," and used commonly, even to feed the household pets. It was made in Staffordshire, England, and sent here to the Colonies in great quantities. It was mostly blue, with pictures of our early buildings, schools, bridges, and so on. Each potter had his own special border of flowers or leaves. Today this pottery, if you can find any, is almost priceless.

Perhaps cupboards will come back. I hope so.

Grandma Said It Good

GRANDMA GOODNESS HAD LIVED IN WEBSTER, MASSA-
chusetts, most of her life except for her last years,
which she spent with us. We were a large family, seven
children, aged from six months to eighteen years.
Although Grandma was in her seventies when she
arrived, she was still able to help with the chores. She
was a tall, angular woman with graying hair rolled up
in a bun atop her head. She died when I was about
twelve years old, and I have never forgotten her and
her way of speech, which was studded with colorful,
sometimes explosive expressions that often gave me
food for thought.

Her quick mind was always equal to a fitting and
sometimes seething phrase, aimed dead center at
whatever caught her eye or ear. I never knew how
many of them she coined herself and how many she
borrowed, but I suspect that many of them were her
very own creations.

A few of them I hear once in a while outside the
immediate family, but many of them have been

handed down from one to another in my own family and are constantly used. Grandmother never wasted words. She always got right to the heart of it, straight to the point with sayings which were full of meaning, though often subtle and somewhat puzzling.

At any show of vanity, she would comment sharply, "Even a coyote got a real pretty tail." Or "Apple butter's pretty thick today." If we complained overmuch: "So you got a bone in your craw." If we boasted: "Braggin' ain't waggin'." Or, "You're warblin' mighty pretty today."

If we were ornery: "Got a barbed-wire tail and ya gotta swing it around." If we were caught spying: "Sneakin' cat never caught a mouse." If we were clumsy: "That one could stub his toe on a mountain."

If we were unkempt: "I've seen better-looking clothes on a scarecrow." If we were slow in thinking: "Don't aggravate your brains." And if we were caught in a lie: "A slick tongue makes a rough life."

A loafer was an "idle hulk." An angry man was "swelled up like a toad." An important person "drags a lot of water."

A bad woman was a "black spider," a bad man a "worthless crow." Parents with too many children were "charting a long course." A hard-hearted woman was "half alligator."

Using initials did not originate with Franklin D. Roosevelt's administration, for Grandma Goodness used them to great advantage. It took me quite a while to find out what G.T.T. meant. But when a neighbor went to prison, I heard Grandma tell his children he had "gone to Texas." I wasn't fooled after that.

An H.F.H. was a "headache for a hippopotamus." And Grandpa had one quite frequently. A B.B. was a "Billy Bullet," a terrific bellyache so named for a man who died from the effects of one. When Grandma saw a storm brewing, she would say, "P.U.!" So the family took to saying, "We are in for a P.U." for "We are in for a spell of bad weather."

Here are more of Grandma's sayings. On the subject of absent-mindedness: "Gone off on another tack." On the subject of sulkiness or brooding: "Take the rag off the bush." At babbling foolishly, we were told, "A Gillygoo lays square eggs."

On religion: "If you live fit, then you're fit to die." On beauty: "A flower needs only the paint God gave it." On resentment: "Don't wear spurs unless you're on a horse." On pretense: "The cheapest shades have the longest tassels."

Grandma disliked fat people, and they were often the target for her caustic comments. "Too bad they don't grow square beans so you could get more on your knife." Or "Too bad they had to put a bone in the ham." Or "He should stack a little more in his head, and less in his stomach."

Thanks to Grandma, all my grandchildren still "go to see Aunt Sally" instead of going to the bathroom. In Grandma's day it was the "privy." She told me how that word originated. It seems that not everyone in those days had an outhouse. Sometimes a neighbor had only the privilege of using one. Soon, "May I have the privilege?" became "May I use the privy?" And so the word was coined.

Grandma had a gift for rhyming, and she directed many of her sharp verses at us. For one whom she thought a simpleton, she'd quote, "Head full of air — he'll get nowhere." On keeping the wrong company: "When a goose pals with a fox, it's the goose gets the knocks."

On worrying: "Go lookin' for trouble, you'll soon find double." On being depressed: "Even an eagle can't always be regal." On apologizing: "If you don't make a cut, you won't have to wrap it up."

On vanity: "Big fish often make small swish." On forgiveness: "Nurse a hurt, 'twill grow for cert." On lending: "Never a lender or borrower be, or you will lose both friend and fee." On thriftiness: "Wear it out, make it do, put a little more water in the stew."

On praise: "Praise to the face is almost disgrace." Of a thin man she'd say, "Who let him in? Just a waste of skin." And of a very small person, "Why, he's just a prick of the thumb, no bigger'n a plum."

Each age seems to find its own peculiar way of expression, but many of the wise words of the past might well be used for the present. And if they only bring a smile, they have served a fine purpose.

Recalling the Nickelodeon

It must have been about 1905 or 1906 when the nickelodeon, the five-cent theater, came to Worcester. I was ten or eleven years old. It was located on Front Street. Some time afterwards, it was known as the Park Theatre. But when it first opened, as the Nickelodeon, it showcased song slides, beautifully colored, often with live models who later became movie stars. Local professional vocalists, billed as "song illustrators," introduced the new ballads to stimulate sales at local stores.

It was a new form of entertainment that was spreading all through the land. It only required a staff of three: a pianist, a projectionist, and the vocalist. Each slide was designed to illustrate one of the very latest hit songs from a play appearing in New York City, or a very popular old favorite.

But, before you were able to enjoy the slides, you were obliged to sit through at least ten minutes of advertising slides, and "mind your manners" slides which offered suggestions such as:

"Please remove your hats."

"Gentlemen, don't spit on the floor."

"Children over six must pay entrance fee."

"Crying babies must be removed."

"Watch out for those hatpins."

"Please don't stick your gum under the seats."

"Food not allowed in the theater."

"No pets allowed."

"Please stand when the U.S. flag comes on the screen."

After a while the theater would darken and the song slides would appear. The singer would stand beside the screen and sing the verses of a popular song, with the appropriate scenes on the screen. They were romantic, colorful, sometimes joyful, sometimes tearful. Then, when the words of the chorus came on the screen, the audience was invited to join in. "Please join in the chorus," then, "Louder! Louder!" the words beckoned.

The singer, now turned choral director, would plead with the audience, "One more time! Whistle, hum, clap your hands, come on!" The audience loved it. Many were determined to buy the sheet music as soon as they left. That, of course, is the way the music publishers had planned it. It was a sort of brainwashing; everyone left singing those songs, and many sat through two or even three performances.

The songs that I remember best were "Wait 'Til the Sun Shines, Nellie," "Down By the Old Mill Stream," "Take Me Out to the Ball Game," "Shine

On, Harvest Moon," "I'm Tying the Leaves So They Won't Come Down," "Won't You Come over to My House?" and "Hello, Central, Give Me Heaven." Many of these songs are still heard occasionally today, though the verses probably are long forgotten.

Local music dealers kept abreast of the times, and when a customer asked for a title he had "heard at the Nickelodeon," the dealer was ready for them. It was a boon, too, for local aspiring young singers. They were in demand both in the Nickelodeon and in the music stores. They weren't paid much, perhaps a dollar for an afternoon or an evening, but it gave them prestige, and took them out of the amateur class.

Among the show business luminaries whose careers began at five-cent theaters were George Jessel, Al Jolson, Sophie Tucker, and many others. George Jessel once remarked that it was a tremendous thrill for him when, as a teenager, he sang "Where Is My (Wand'ring) Boy Tonight?" The illustrations for the song depicted a young man at the bar of a saloon, and showed the mother at a window weeping. It was just too much for the audience. They, too, wept with her.

I recall seeing Francis X. Bushman in one of these early song slides. Old-timers will remember that handsome face. As a rule the featured couple were limited to holding hands, and looking into each other's eyes. If they did kiss, it was of short duration. There were no hot, lurid love scenes. Everything was calm, beautiful, and peaceful: flowering bushes, green grass, blue water, and floating white clouds.

Many of the songs were tearjerkers. One that always caused me to weep buckets was "The Little Lost Child." The scene was a sweet little golden-haired child sobbing in the arms of a policeman. Other heartbreakers included "Why Doesn't Santa Claus Go Next Door?" and "The Flower of Singapore," which showed a lovely girl in a sad state, after a drinking bout.

Many of the names of those long-ago models for those slides are still remembered. Norma Talmadge was only fourteen years of age when she started modeling. In many of the old music slides I recall her—in a lovely yellow dress and picture hat, in "Any Old Time," dancing with a boy in a field of roses. Later, she applied for work in motion pictures (then called "flicks") at Vitagraph's studio in Brooklyn. She started what was to become a twenty-year career in pictures at five dollars a day.

Anita Stewart also joined Vitagraph after posing for song slides. For some reason, many of the motion picture stars wanted to forget about their early modeling work in song slides, as though it were unmentionable or disgraceful. Maybe it was the cheap admittance price. Later on, the price went to a dime, and the name "Nickelodeon" vanished.

Very short movies soon appeared. They lasted only fifteen minutes or less, and were added to the song slide program. I recall one starring Mary Pickford. She had cut off her beautiful hair to buy a watch for her husband. And he had sold his coat to buy her a comb for her hair. Very sad.

Over the course of about twenty years, thousands of these song slides were made in the United States. Unfortunately, most of them were destroyed. These relics of nickelodeons and vaudeville are among the scarcest memorabilia of the theater. There was a chance discovery of a small cache of these old slides thirty years ago, in St. Louis, Missouri.

It seems that when the last of the nickelodeons had either closed or changed over into "flick" theaters, offering multireel feature films, the lovely song slides were no longer wanted. When opulent picture palaces came into being, the song slides were considered "old hat." Unable to be sold, they must have been dumped into the trash.

The Grand Old Fourth

WHEN I WAS YOUNG THE FOURTH OF JULY WAS THE grandest day in all the year. No self-respecting kid would be caught in bed the night before, and as soon as the midnight bells had stopped ringing, the racket would set off all the dogs in town.

All the older kids had giant firecrackers as well as the little strings of "ladyfingers" and torpedoes, cannons, and ammunition for sending tin cans and wash buckets skyward. All the smaller kids had cap guns, peashooters, and noisemakers. And they were up with the sun to celebrate the day.

On the great day itself, there were parades, glorious parades, with all the Civil War veterans in their old uniforms, and their old banners waving in the wind. There were picnics, speeches, and drills on the common, and patriotic demonstrations of all kinds. There was a special committee for municipal jubilations, and they did themselves proud every year.

On the street facing the common, stalls were set up. Here you could buy refreshments throughout the day—lemonade to quench those throats hoarse from yelling, cotton candy, sticky peppermint sticks, huge homemade doughnuts, pies and cakes, and big crusty sandwiches of ham and chicken and beef. And catchpenny prizes such as bisque dolls and wooden jumping jacks to win when playing the games.

Early in the morning, as soon as the sun came up, the National Guard discharged a National Salute. Three big bangs, and the day had started. In an hour a big crowd had gathered. And the American Brass Band rode in followed by the chief marshal with all his aides. Then the United Artillery in brilliant blue uniforms, all carrying muskets, then the Light Infantry, then the Cadets, and on and on. The big parade was forming.

There were a great many carriages carrying all the important officials of the day, besides the members of the city council, and the staff of the governor, the day's orators, and other luminaries. There were many bands all in bright uniforms, some with white leggings and some with green jackets and green felt hats with white feathers. Oh! They were wonderful to see, and their instruments were shined up so that they gleamed and glistened in the sun.

The procession moved out right on time, and the boom, boom, boom and the clang, clang, clang was a marvelous sound. The route was long, but we ran along with them to the end; and when they disbanded in a big field for the exercises to take place, we were right there beside them and not a bit tired. The units cheered each other, the big flags were put aside for the time being, and the exercises began.

First, a lovely schoolgirl of about sixteen years of age sang "My Country 'Tis of Thee" in a thin, sweet voice that brought tears to the eyes. Then a schoolboy read the Declaration of Independence. Then came the mayor's speech, followed by a chorus of schoolchildren. Now came a breaking out of cap-gun reports, with parents not being able to keep the small children silent much longer. But they were soon hushed up so that the other part of the program could go on.

At noon there was a series of cannon salutes on the old common, a ringing of church bells, and a feast for all the officials set up in a tent nearby. At the same time there were several picnic groups in various parts of the city, and mothers and fathers, laden with baskets of food, were rounding up their offspring to cart them off to the eating places.

About three o'clock there was a grand parade of all the fire equipment, all polished up for the occasion, the big silver "steamer" exhaling great clouds of steam and gleaming like silver. The brave firemen, in bright new red uniforms, perched atop their wagons as proud as proud could be. It was an exciting display. We loved it. But how we worried. Suppose there was a fire? But there was none, and the laddies put on a brave show jumping and leaping into the air.

Now it was already getting dark, the sun slowly sinking. And the very best part of the day was ahead of us: the fireworks display and the bonfire. Men had worked all day while we were enjoying ourselves, setting up the grand fireworks display. There were skyrockets, whirling pinwheels, "flowerpots," Roman candles with not only one but seven and eight balls of fire coming forth.

There were Bengal lights that illuminated the whole field and mammoth torpedoes that stung the ears. There were battery pieces, and "picture" displays that made us gasp in admiration; there stood the American flag in gorgeous color and Uncle Sam in full dress.

But the *pièce de résistance,* the ultimate, the chilling and delightfully horrifying end, was the bombshells. They shrieked, they whistled, they screamed as they went upward and upward, high into the sky, only to burst with a terrific explosion of golden stars that took our breath away.

That was our glorious and wonderful Fourth seventy-five years ago. A day to remember all our lives. Have we lost it? Forever?

Morality in the Early 1900s

THE VICTORIAN IDEAS OF MORALITY SEEM STRANGE TO us now, and the views of propriety mysterious. Looking back, I believe there was a great deal of pretense and unreality in Victorian dos and don'ts, even a deliberate hypocrisy. For many of those old rules now seem quite stupid, and some of the books that were banned seem as tame as the Bobbsey Twins.

Very early in my life I was often given the role of chaperone to courting couples. My oldest sister, for instance, was just starting to have "beaux." They would sit on the sofa in the parlor, with the door wide open of course, and my father would say, "You, Jen, go and sit in there with them." It was very unusual for a courting couple to be left by themselves.

On one occasion, a young man arrived before my sister was ready to receive him. She was in her room, curling the fringe on her forehead with a curling iron held over the gas jet. I was directed to "go in there and talk to him nicely until your sister comes down." Soon, she appeared with her fringe curled very prettily. I had been entertaining him by telling him that he was the fifth caller she had that week, whereupon he strode to the mantle over the fireplace and lowered his head down over his folded arms in anguish. And that is how she found him. He looked at her and said, "My heart is broken." I thought he was disgustingly silly.

I suppose my father thought I'd be a little less of a restraint than a grown person would be, but I doubt it. I'm sure they hated me and surely they must have sensed my disgust whenever he squeezed her hand, or looked into her eyes and sighed. It never went any further than that.

I myself was about fourteen years old when my first boyfriend came to visit (though they were never called by that term at that time—they were "beaux"). He was in the same grade as I was in grammar school, the last, or ninth grade, which would now be junior high school. He would walk by the house, see me sitting on the front steps, and join me. At nine o'clock sharp, my father would come to the front door and say, "Come, children, time for bed. Time for you to go home now, son." And he'd jump up and go. This went on for four years, though in cold weather we'd go in and sit where it was warm. Then one evening Papa caught us with our arms around each other, and told us, "I guess you children better get married." So we did.

We never, in our time, used the word "sex." That word was used only to designate the gender of a person. We might say a girl was "fast" or "man-crazy," but "sexy," never. And of course, the word "gay" simply meant a very, very happy person or event. An "affair" was just a happening, and had nothing to do with love.

I was very easily shocked. For instance, I once saw one of my uncles grab my aunt (his wife), and kiss her heartily. I ran away from them in absolute horror of this unprecedented orgy. My cheeks flushed, and I was ashamed of them. In my mind, it was a revolting scene. People never kissed in public. I once read in a book of old early Puritan laws that a man could be fined five shillings for kissing his wife in public. So, at the age of eight years, I must have been living in a Puritan age.

When I was about nine or ten, I was taken to see the play *Charley's Aunt*. When I saw the young man come on the stage dressed in female clothes and a wig, and with rouge on his cheeks, petticoats lifted high to show his legs and underpants, I was so shocked I trembled. I closed my eyes. I thought it was a vulgar scene, and not at all funny. What a little prude I must have been.

Children who were well brought up were shielded from hearing anything about birth, or anything to do with the sexes, until marriage. I was as curious as most children, and often annoyed my mother with questions; but the answers were always baffling, and must have been very clever also, as I never learned anything from them.

When Aunt Mary was very large with child, I asked

my mother why she was so big. My mother answered,
"Oh, she's wearing her bustle in front for a change." I
once asked her, when I was about eight years old, why
I had that little button in the middle of my tummy.
She said, "That is where God finished you." And
from then on, I had a visual image of God tying up
one baby, and starting in on another.

I recall the time when we were visiting relatives,
and I was put in the same room as my Aunt Emma.
She stood by the side of the bed after I was in it, and
slowly removed her clothing until she was stark naked. She was very fat and bulgy. I was only about
three or four years old, and I had never seen *a naked
person* before. I shrieked and ran out of the room,
appalled at so much flesh in sight. I'm sure my aunt
did not have much affection for me after that episode.

Nudity was considered a sin, and we were taught
to undress under our nighties, and dress up under
them also. Even a display of ankles in an adult female
was considered very vulgar. I remember the lovely
summer day when my father took us boating on Lake
Quinsigamond. We passed by a group of young boys
swimming as naked as the Lord had made them. My
father yelled at us, "Close your eyes, girls, don't
look!" and he rowed quickly past. It must have been a
lovely sight, those thin pink naked boys, dashing in
and out of the water, and dancing on the lush, green
grass, amid flowering bushes and singing birds.

In our home as in most homes of that period, we
had a stereopticon and many slides to be shown

through it. This was a double-view curved glass on a long handle. Some of the slides were kept separate, for adult viewing only. Once, when I was alone in the house, I got hold of these slides, took them to my room, and looked at them. The wildest one I remember was a scene of a servant with only a very short slip on, titled "Serving the tomatoes undressed."

There was one uncle who was very jovial, and he always had a funny story to tell us, or a cute rhyme to quote. But my mother always warned him to "be careful." And sometimes she scolded him afterwards, saying "it was not quite suitable." One evening he quoted Cowper's "Epitaph on a Hare." It went like this:

> *A turkey carpet was his lawn,*
> *Whereon he loved to bound;*
> *To skip and gambol like a fawn,*
> *And swing his rump around.*

"What's a 'rump'?" I asked. My mother was quite angry with my uncle. "That is a very vulgar poem to recite to children," she said, "but if you must know, a 'rump' is the back part of an animal. And it is a word that you must never use." She did not explain what word I should use in its place, but I doubt that she would have wanted me to use the proper word.

Once I asked my mother why our neighbor's daughter had a baby, and she was not married. My mother said, "That is none of your business." "Well,"

I said, "she wasn't very polite, was she?" And mother
said, "No, it was not polite."

Certainly the rules of propriety in the early 1900s
were puzzling, and made life very complex for a
child. I'm sure an eight-year-old child today asking
such questions would be considered somewhat re-
tarded. And it seems strange to me that children of
that day, surely just as intelligent, would accept, without question, the unrealistic moral values of that time.
They were foolish rules for an age that will never
return.

Valentine Memory from 1916

I LOVE HATS. I'VE ALWAYS LOVED HATS. AND THIS HAT was a dream hat. The kind of a hat I had always wanted. It was in the window of Lowell's Hat Emporium on Main Street, Worcester. It was the loveliest shade of blue, made of a soft suedelike material, with a narrow brim, curved down a little in the front, and a tiny white feather on the side: smart-looking, elegant, yet simple.

I stood with my face pressed against the glass. Oh, I'd give anything to have that hat. But I knew I must not think of it. We had only been married for a little more than a year, V.J. and I, and now he was out of work. Business was not good, so he had been laid off, being the last one hired. We were living in a brand-new apartment building on Madison Street in Worcester, in a cozy little three-room apartment, all nicely furnished, for only fifteen dollars a month.

V.J. was desperately looking for work, standing in long lines every day in the cold and wind, with no success.

It was Valentine's Day — the year, 1916. I had spent the previous evening making a valentine for V.J. Bits of lace and tiny red hearts, and a larger heart which opened to reveal a little poem of my own, and the words, "To One I Love." I had presented it to him this morning, but he only said, "Thank you." And he had nothing for me. I was very hurt. He had always given me a box of chocolates, decorated with ribbons, or a box of pretty handkerchiefs. "Perhaps he still will," I thought, but knew he wouldn't. It wasn't the money, for even a penny valentine would have pleased me.

This late afternoon, I was on my way home from work. A friend had succeeded in getting me a job as sales clerk in Barnard Sumner and Putnam, a department store on Main Street. I had just been paid my weekly salary of eighteen dollars, and I was window-shopping, the streets crowded, many of the stores still open, windows still brightly lit up.

I knew I should hurry home to get supper, but I just stood there admiring that hat. I knew it would look nice on me. It would make me feel confident and proud. After all, V.J. just might ask me to go out tonight, and he would be very proud of me with that hat on. Why didn't I go in and try it on, just for fun? Of course, I could not afford to buy it. I could see the price tag — it was fifteen dollars, far more than I had ever paid for a hat. But, certainly, it was harmless just to try it on. If it didn't look good on me, then I could forget about it.

I went into the shop, walking on deep crimson carpeting, and sat in a chair by the window, waiting for a clerk. Soon, a buxom woman came over and asked, "What can I do for you?" I pointed. "That blue hat in the window. I just want to try it on."

She reached in the window for it, and handed it to me with a frosty smile. I sat before a mirror and adjusted it on my head, tipping the brim a little more, pulling a stray curl out over my forehead. I was delighted to see that it looked just as good on me as I thought it would, just as good as on the mannequin.

The saleswoman was really smiling now. "It's very, very becoming," she said. "You'd be foolish not to buy that hat. It was made for you." I knew I should, too, but I also knew I shouldn't. And my thoughts took another jump. Perhaps V.J. would like it so much, he would be glad I bought it. "Could I change it if my husband doesn't like it?" I asked.

"Of course, no problem," she answered. I thought with pleasure of walking out with V.J. that evening and then I could take it back in the morning, if he thought it was too expensive. "I'll take it," I said, and soon I was walking out of the store with the hat in a lovely round hatbox.

I was elated at first, but then I became fearful. I argued with myself all the way home. After all, it was my own money. And he hadn't given me a valentine gift. And we did still have a few dollars in the bank. We weren't absolutely penniless. But I had a feeling that I was in trouble. I stopped on the way at the

Mohican Market on Franklin Street to buy two pork chops and a few vegetables, and that took almost another dollar. The butcher smiled at me and threw in a soupbone with a little meat on it. Now I could get V.J. a nice hot supper, but I still hoped we would go out.

Arriving home, I pressed the elevator button, heading for our top-floor apartment. When I opened the door to the apartment, I saw that V.J. was sitting by the table lamp, reading the evening paper, turned to the want ads. Slumped down in his chair, he looked tired, discouraged. "Hi, V.J.," I said cheerfully.

He looked up. "Hi, Jen." His usual high spirits seemed to have left him completely. Then he saw the package. "What's in the Mohican bag? Are you keeping me now? And what's in the box? Are they giving away hats somewhere?" That was a bad beginning, I knew.

"Let's go out and eat tonight," I said. "It's Valentine's Day."

He shouted at me. "With what?"

"I have two bucks here," I said. "We can get dollar dinners at the Capitol Cafe." I opened the hatbox and put on the hat. "Wouldn't you like to step out with me tonight?" I walked around and wiggled my hips a little. I batted my eyelashes at him. His reaction was nothing like what I expected. He stared at me, his fine brown eyes almost bulging. "Don't tell me you bought a hat and me out of work! How much did it cost?" I told him.

He jumped up from his chair. "Fifteen dollars! And I thought I had a sensible wife. You little fool!" I felt as though he had slapped me. V.J. is a Sagittarius, and they are very frank and often brutally outspoken. But it was the first time he had ever spoken to me that way. I am a Gemini, and we are very sensitive. I started to cry. But that seemed to infuriate him even more.

"Get it out of my sight," he shouted, and he snatched the hat from my head and threw it to the far corner of the room.

I picked up the hat. It was crushed, the price tag was torn off, and there was a tiny tear in it. Now, I thought, I cannot return it. But I said, to try to pacify him, "I'll try to return it in the morning." He didn't answer. His face was white, his lips grim.

I left the room, smoothing the hat, almost caressing it. I put it back in the box and went back to the kitchen to start supper. "Don't cook for me," said V.J. "I don't want any supper." Finally the good smells got to him and he did eat, but silently. And he went to bed in silence, his eyes still hard, his lips still grim. That night I prayed: "Please, God, don't let him leave me." And I promised myself I would rise early, repair the hat, fix him a good breakfast, then return the hat to the store.

The next morning came, cold and windy. Though it was still dark, V.J. was dressed and ready to leave. He slammed the door as he left: no good-bye, no kiss, nothing. I repaired the hat, and it looked good as new.

I put it on once more. And a thought came to me. Why couldn't I wear it to the shop and put it back in the box just before I went in? Again, I couldn't resist. I donned my very best coat, a white chinchilla, and tied a blue chiffon scarf around my neck. The hat looked fabulous with it. And I left.

Most stores were just opening, and Main Street was crowded. I passed the Boston store, and waved to a friend. "My," she said, "you look terrific this morning." I walked by Easton's, its window still full of beautiful valentines, and I felt the hurt again. I thought of my school years when I received so many lovely valentines, and tears came to my eyes.

Then I saw a line standing at a men's clothing shop where there was a sign reading, CLERK WANTED. And I saw him, V.J., about halfway down the line. I turned quickly, but he had already seen me, so I felt I must go speak to him. He glared at me; he glared at the hat. Just as I turned again to leave, a gust of wind took the hat from my head and whirled it through the air, and it landed at the feet of a tall man standing at the door of the shop. He had been watching us.

He picked it up, handed it to me with a gallant bow, and said, "It would be tragic for you to lose this lovely hat. It is very becoming." Then he asked, "Is that your husband you were talking to?" I said, "Yes," thanked him, and left. On reaching the hat shop, I took off the hat, put it back in the box, and returned it with no trouble, but with a pang in my heart, as though I had parted with all my worldly wealth.

When I arrived home that day, the apartment was empty. I put the meatbone on to cook, feeling bad for myself. Suddenly, the door flew open and V.J. walked in. In one hand he held a huge white envelope—in the other, a hatbox. The hatbox! Was I dreaming?

"Janey," he shouted, his eyes shining. "You'll never believe it, because I can't believe it! I've got a job. A good job. A steady job. With good pay. And all because of you. He liked you. He liked your hat. He asked me questions and he liked my answers. And he said I must be a heck of a guy to get a girl like you. I bought back the hat. It brought me luck. And here's your valentine. I'm so sorry, honey. I was a brute. Will you forgive me? And take that pot off the stove. We're eating out. And not at the Capitol Cafe, but at Putnam and Thurston's."

Tears were in my eyes again, tears of happiness. I am a Gemini, and Geminis cry when we're happy.

Sweet Songs of Yesteryear

"I HEAR AMERICA SINGING," WALT WHITMAN WROTE in 1860. In 1904, when I was a small child, the air was full of music: tinkling pianos, squeaking fiddles, and quavering voices.

I remember the old songs, and the sheet music in the Sunday papers. We would gather around the upright piano to try them out.

In the days before radio and television, it was a very special kind of music, sometimes very sad, sometimes very joyous, unsophisticated and homely; filled with crude sentiment or crude humor, which often caused maidenly blushes or womanly tears.

There is a lot of bad music around today, and there was a lot of bad music around then. It might even have been worse. It seems America must, at times, have a tin ear.

Waltzes, polkas, and quadrilles were all the rage. Publishers soon found out that if they gave their sheet music lurid covers, it would sell much better. And if they made up the lyrics based on popular subjects of the day, it sold quickly. Life was dull, and people were music-mad.

Even tragedies of the day were written into music. In 1862, when the ship *Golden Gate* sank while burning off the coast of Mexico, a song was written describing the rescue of a child from the wreck.

> *On deck there is terror and agony wild.*
> *"The ship is on fire!" is the ominous sound.*
> *And pleading for life, hear a motherless child,*
> *"Oh! Save me! Please do! I don't want to be drowned!"*

Grandma had a copy of this music with its cover depicting the burning ship in glowing, vivid color, and she cherished it.

Another "oldie" (1868) was "The Charming Young Widow I Met in the Train." This was a story of a young man who met a lovely widow on a train in Vermont. She asked him to hold her baby, then disappeared. Then he found out she had robbed him of his wallet and watch.

> *I live in Vermont and one morning last summer*
> *A letter informed me my Uncle was dead,*
> *And also requested I'd come down to Boston*
> *As he left me a large sum of money it said;*
> *Of course I determ'd on making the journey*
> *And to book myself by the "first class" I was fain,*
> *Though had I gone "second" I had never encountered*
> *The charming young widow I met in the train.*

There was "The Drummer Boy of Shiloh" and

"Homeless Tonight" and "The Faithful Engineer," all sad songs. These were all before my time, but Grandma still sung them, and remembered most of the words.

The songs of my time were the songs my mother used to sing as she went about her household chores. She had a lovely thin, sweet voice, and I loved to hear her.

These songs were livelier, mostly happy songs, but there were a few sad ones, too. My favorite was "Flow Gently, Sweet Afton." A haunting melody, and though I am a monotone, I still try to sing it: "Flow gently, sweet Afton, among thy green braes . . ."

There was the time of an epidemic of scarlet fever, when we children were all bedded down with it. Mother nursed us back to health, singing to us while she tended to us, all her favorites: "Kathleen Mavourneen," "Walking Nellie Home," "The Little Brown Jug," "The Harp That Once, Thro' Tara's Halls," "The Flying Trapeze," "Comin' Through the Rye," "Two Little Girls in Blue," and many, many others.

Some of these songs lived on to become the folk music of America. One famous survivor, "The Flying Trapeze" (mid-1800s), became a favorite with circus clowns. Later on it became popular with singer Rudy Vallee. Today it is still familiar with singers everywhere.

Quite recently, I heard a parody of that song called "What's Become of My Love?" A girl was substituted for the man in the song:

She floats through the air with the greatest of ease.
You'd think her a man on the flying trapeze.
She does all the work while he takes his ease.
And that's what became of my love.

Some songs never die, and this seems to be one of them.

I remember one song that was sung everywhere when I was a little girl, "Matilda Toots." It was a horrible song which inspired many, many parodies. Often, the children were sent from the room when they were sung.

In pre-Freudian days, when an ankle was an aphrodisiac, "Matilda" was a racy song. It seems the heroine was having her boots laced up when she fell over backwards.

Oh! Matilda Toots, you should have seen her boots.
On the ice they looked so nice,
But when she fell over, you should have looked twice!

When I was a teenager, the songs were much different. And whereas today's songs seem to come and go quickly, songs in that day seemed to last. They were on everyone's tongue, everywhere.

Department stores had a "music room" where people gathered to hear the latest songs sung. Ice-cream parlors, too, employed singers and piano players to sing the latest hits from the new musicals while you sat at a little table and spooned up your sundae.

Most of the songs were lively and gay. Among the most popular: "Won't You Come Over to My House?" "Slidin' Down My Cellar Door," "Whistle and I'll Come to You," "Bill Bailey, Won't You Please Come Home?" "In the Shade of the Old Apple Tree," "Sweet Georgia Brown," "Call Me Up Some Rainy Afternoon," "Down by the Old Mill Stream," and so many others.

But there were some sad songs, too: "The Vacant Chair," "I'm Tying the Leaves So They Won't Come Down, So Nellie Won't Go Away," "Hello Central, Give Me Heaven," "Sweet Rosie O'Grady," and "How Green Was My Valley." We shed tears over those songs. In happy times, people sang sad songs.

Both my sisters had beautiful voices, and often sang in public. When sister Rose sang "A Perfect Day," the room was hushed and still. It became a classic. As did "The Kashmiri Song (Pale Hands I Loved Beside the Shalimar)." I loved that one, and I still do. Those old songs seem to linger, sweet and fragrant in the mind.

There were crazy songs too— "Yes! We Have No Bananas," that one is still hanging around. And "Mairzy Doats, and Dozy Doats, and Liddle Lamzy Divey." That made no sense until you studied it. Then it was still crazy. "Mares eat oats, and does eat oats, and little lambs eat ivy." But it was a fun song, as was "Under the Coconut Tree (Won't You Come and Dance with Me?)."

I find great pleasure in the elusive phantoms of old

memories and old songs. I enjoy them without too much sadness or recrimination or regrets. The heart and mind can relive them again and again and again. A good song never dies.

My Early Venture
in Real Estate

I REMEMBER CLEARLY THE DAY I SAW THE AD THAT changed my life. I had been happily married for about two years, and we had a baby girl about one year old. But we were living in a top floor tenement in the type of house called a "three-decker," and we were not happy with that kind of living. The landlady was a tyrant who supervised my every motion. We wanted a home very badly.

The ad read like this. "For Sale. A 2-family house, needing repairs. Will sell to a handy man needing a home. Little capital needed. Mr. M———."

Well, here was our big chance. It seemed the ad was written just for us. My husband, Victor, was very handy. He could fix anything. We certainly needed a home, and we had little capital. In fact, we had nothing. Only our youth, health, and sincerity.

The very next day I went to call on Mr. M. He was seated at his desk in his office, a short, rather corpulent man with a balding head but thick, shaggy black eyebrows, and a beaky nose.

I was very small for my age and wore my hair short, in ringlets about my face. I'm sure I looked more like a grammar school student than a wife and mother. Mr. M. looked rather astonished.

"What can I do for you, kid?" he asked. I had the newspaper clipping clutched in my hand. I held it up.

"I'd like to know how much this house is," I answered.

"You—you—you," he stuttered, "you mean you want to buy this house?"

"That's right," I said. "My husband and I would like to buy it if the price is right. He is very handy, and we need a home very badly."

"How old are you?" he asked. Then questioned me further. "How long have you been married? Where do you live?" Then the inevitable question. "How much money do you have?"

I answered all his questions including the last one. "We don't have any money at all." He stared at me with open mouth.

"You want I should GIVE you the house?" he asked. I mimicked him: "You want we should work for nothing?" I was trembling, but trying to be bold. I went into the speech I had prepared on the way.

"We are young and healthy. We need a home. If you turn the deed over to us, we will work very hard. If, at the end of a year, we have not paid as per contract, or done enough work, you could foreclose the mortgage. So how can you lose? Please! Try us."

Mr. M. stroked his chin. Then he got up and paced the floor.

"If I agree, what are you going to use for money? How are you going to make repairs?"

"I thought you might lend us the first money we need," I said.

Mr. M. threw back his head and let out a roar of laughter. "You sure have guts, kid," he said, "and I'll be darned if I'm just not going to do it, though I must be out of my mind."

He walked over to a shelf and took some pictures from it. "This is the house. What do you think of it?" My heart sank. The lines of the house were good. But everything sagged — the doors, the shutters, the roof. Even the chimney sagged. The house was probably white once, but was now a dingy gray, and in some places had no paint left at all.

"It's pretty bad," I said, "but"—I hastened to add— "it's not hopeless. I'm sure it can be fixed up." I knew he had shown me those pictures to discourage me. To shock me. But I spoke casually. "What is the price?"

He named it. "Forty-five hundred dollars. And that is dirt cheap." I nodded. "I'd like to see it." "Come on," he said. And he led me out to his old Ford. The house was on top of a hill, one of many old Victorian houses. I was glad he had shown me the pictures. I knew what to expect. But I knew I must put all negative thoughts aside. It was our only chance. It was only a beginning, a steppingstone to the house of my dreams.

I found out that there had been a fire in the two back bedrooms. The walls were slightly scorched and had not been repaired, so the tenants were not paying the rent. They had been throwing their trash in the yard, and it was a mess. They allowed me to go in and look around, but they were quick to show me all the flaws. They told me that I would be "nuts" to buy that place at any price: But I saw some things I liked. The parlor was large and sunny. The windows were "12 over 12," small panes. The front door had once been beautiful, and could be made beautiful again. The kitchen was sunny too, and had lots of cabinets. The bathroom was not bad. It only needed a good scrubbing and prettying up. The faucets worked fine. The water tasted good. The walls needed papering, but the plaster was firm. The foundation of the house seemed to be strong, and the roof leaked only in a few spots.

It was an ethnic neighborhood, once prestigious, but now fallen into neglect. There were quite a few Irish and Armenians, a sprinkling of Italians, a few Jewish families, and a few first residents, real Yankees, still lived there. It was a quiet neighborhood, though I found out after we moved there that there could be disturbances. Tom Murphy might come weaving down the street on pay night, singing merrily, but on his way home. Shrill shrieks might be heard in the middle of the night, and you knew Mrs. Renski or Mrs. Katz was having a baby.

And Oh! the heavenly odors in the air. The fat sausages, the blintzes, the shish kebabs, the pork pies. And the neighbors were so generous. Just mention that something smelled good, and very soon a sample would arrive at your door. They were wonderful people. But I found all that out afterwards.

But there was one event that clinched my decision to give Mr. M. a quick, firm answer: "Yes! I want it." Next door to the house was a little variety store, owned by a little Jewish man named Abe. He came out to greet me. He shook my hand and told me he was impressed with my youth and my courage. He told me I could use his phone, and offered me a charge account until we got started. He was the kindest man I ever knew. And he kept his word.

The next day Mr. M. met with my husband and me to discuss details and clauses. We signed papers. The next week I held the mortgage to the house in my hand, and in my purse was a hundred dollars in cash to buy the first supplies for repairs. *We* were the owners of a house. We were on our way.

We had trials and tribulations with that house. And we had fun, too. And made wonderful friends.

The first year we cleared the yard, planted grass seed, and started a garden. We papered all the rooms, upstairs and down. We painted the kitchen walls, put down new linoleum, painted the cabinets, renovated the bathrooms.

At the end of the second year we had painted the house, white with green shutters. A new chimney, new heating system, and wall-to-wall carpeting. Everything was clean and beautiful. Then we put the house up for sale. After paying off all our obligations, we still made a handsome profit. And we bought our "dream house."

Never Wipe Your Nose
on Your Coat Sleeve

A NUMBER OF YEARS AGO—I THINK ABOUT 1962—IT was "Open House" Day in Edgartown, Martha's Vineyard. I visited Emily Post as she sat in the garden of her lovely home.

Aging, but gracious and lovely as ever, she poured tea in dainty china cups as she spoke to us on the derelict manners of the day. But contrary to modern thought, Emily Post did not write the first book on etiquette—there have been many of them over the years. I've been leafing through one that is a little gem.

The title is *The Young Lady's Friend,* from 1861. "By a Young Lady" is all that appears on the flyleaf. But lovely, gracious Emily would have flipped—indeed would have been staggered—at the pearls of wisdom and sage advice in this little book.

"If you must spit, spit in a corner, so that your

hostess will not see you" is one perfectly serious injunction.

And there's this other little dandy. "If a gentleman wishes to admire a breastpin or a chain around your neck, never allow him to put his hand out to touch it, but remove it from your person, and hand it to him to inspect. Never allow him to touch anything on your person for gentlemen can be very tricky in this respect."

This book also advises girls, "Riding in a chaise" (that's a wagon, girls, not a couch) "alone with a gentleman, is a pleasure that should be reserved for the man you intend to marry and should never happen with a common acquaintance. Doing such things could ruin your reputation for life and you would deserve it." So there!

There is another little book that I have been allowed to see and read. Fragile with age, pages yellow and foxed, still it is much more up to date, for this one was published only one hundred years ago. On the flyleaf is a lovely hand-colored rose and the words, *Letters To A Young Lady On A Variety of Subjects*, by Rev. John Bennett, Brattleboro, Vermont, "Calculated to Improve The Heart, To Form Good Manners, And To Enlighten The Mind. Dedicated To Our Fair Daughters, The Polished Cornerstones Of the Temple Of God."

The letters are rather dry reading, weak and superficial in their arguments, given mostly to proper dress, proper conduct, and application to studies. But once in a while there is a real gem, hardly seeming to come from a minister of the gospel. "A woman without love is a rose-less thorn, a winter without spring, a summer without warmth," he laments. "Such a woman has no softness, her bosom is unyielding, her soul denying and void."

Or take this passage from Letter IV. "It has been said that every woman is a rake at heart. This sentence is severe, but it must be admitted that there is some truth to it. I believe there is some good in every woman, no matter how bad, but I must confess to having been shaken up by many of them. I blush at their boldness. Showing their ankles, shamelessly. Embracing in public — shocking!"

In an 1894 magazine, there was published an article called, "How Are Your Horse-car Manners?" Among other things it says: "A few years ago it was a rare thing to see a woman standing in a horse-car. Now-a-days, nothing is more common than to see delicate ladies clinging to the straps. They totter and sway, almost landing in the laps of the so-called gentlemen. One might even be pregnant. A horrible thought. This is a shameful thing, and I hope one day to see one of the ladies pummel one with her umbrella."

That was in the late 1800s. In the early 1800s (1801), in a magazine of the day called *Godey's Ladies' Book*, a treatise on "How to Bathe Correctly" stated: "Draw the tub to a warm place, near the stove if possible. Put in a handful of soft soap and a few drops of oil of cloves or peppermint. Be sure the doors are locked. Remove your clothes, except stockings." (It's true, I swear it.) "Sit in the tub and rub the soap all over between toes. Remove towel and put on your Mother Hubbard and put stockings back on. Never, never, walk naked around the house. Not only that you might catch cold, but someone could walk in."

In the field of masculine manners, *Lord Chesterfield's Letters* were referred to a great deal by magazine and newspaper editors in the late 1800s. They were slanted for gentlemen only of course, but the ladies read them eagerly, hoping to get a thrill from them. The following is from one of these letters. "On a very hot day a gentleman may remove his coat if he feels faint, but must never, never, remove his vest. He may loosen his tie but never remove it."

From the same source: "Always brown shoes with brown suit, black shoes with black suit. Anything else is careless dressing." Also, "Gentlemen should never make unseemly noises from inside. There is no excuse for this." And this gem: "A gentleman should always offer a lady his coat if she is cold."

About a hundred years ago, the *Franklin Democrat,* published in Greenfield, printed a little essay on etiquette for the young man and his father. "A man who wipes his nose on his coatsleeve is scarcely a gentleman," said this authority. "Buttons should be sewed on the edge of the sleeve to prevent this awful thing from happening.

"Also, if a gentleman's lady is talking too much, he

should place his hand over her mouth, gently. This is permissible, but he should never shout at her, or hit her even slightly."

Mrs. Frank Leslie, in *Rents in Our Robes,* advised women in the middle 1800s: "An Indian will always be an Indian. But remember that after he was induced to wear his shirt inside his leggings, he became less wild. Therefore, please place plenty of buttons on the waistbands of your man's pantaloons, so that his shirt will not stray outside, and you will find him more amenable to law and order."

One publication, *Advice to Young Marrieds,* in the *Worcester Spy,* 1892, has some advice that should really stun you: "Ladies, have pity on your poor tired husband when he comes home from work. Keep yourselves covered up so as not to tempt him to sin. Brew him weak tea in the winter and cold in the summer. Sing hymns with him at night, and read, out loud, to him bits from good books, but never lurid novels."

Gay's Encyclopedia was very popular in the early 1900s, "A Book For All The People." It gave rules for writing a love letter that would be a dilly. You could also learn to be a lawyer or a doctor. It covered everything: how to help with childbirth, bookkeeping, housekeeping, winemaking, beer brewing, entertainment, history, jokes, and flowing penmanship. It even told how to play an organ.

There were pages of cooking "receipts," as they were called then. And pages of homemade medicines. Some of them were really weird. For instance, a rule for a cold cure: "Take a live frog, pop it in boiling water, boil 15 minutes. Mash it, add a little spirits of nitre, a half-cup of molasses and teaspoon of soda. Stir well, and take one tablespoon every hour." Who wouldn't rather have a cold?

When the Big Show
Came to Town

I HAVE ALWAYS BEEN FASCINATED WITH THE CIRCUS AND
circus people. As our home was situated right on the
edge of the fairgrounds where they pitched their big
tent each year, I had the opportunity to watch their
activities, and to become acquainted with the performers. It was very exciting. We would all get up in
very early morning to watch them come in. My oldest
son, David, would disappear, and we wouldn't see
him for the rest of the day. The advance men came in
the middle of the night to set up the stakes for the big
tent, and to set up the stoves and start the meals.

Then suddenly, the whole big show arrived—the
big open wagons with the lions, tigers, and seals, the
elephants, the coaches, the horses, the private cars.
There was frantic, furious screaming, yelling, rush-
ing, running; it was a madhouse. But finally, it was
done and ready, and the workers would be eating
peacefully, the animals would be fed, and the girls

would get into costume. The big parade would be starting before noontime.

Many of the performers came to my door to ask little favors — to use the phone for personal reasons, or to get some hot water, a safety pin or a needle, a few ice cubes. The sideshow people especially, for they seemed to be apart from the regular performers, and to have more time on their hands. I got to know Sally, the fat lady, quite well. Until recently, I had her picture in my wallet. She was a very sweet, kind person, not a big eater — her accumulation of fat was due to a glandular illness. She weighed over four hundred pounds and could not walk without crutches, and her one great wish was to be normal.

I also spoke to Mr. and Mrs. Tom Thumb several times. They were not the real Tom Thumbs, and in fact, they were not even married, but were very good friends. These very small people traveled in a special coach made for them with two baby cribs, two tiny chairs, a little stove, and two closets. They hated to be called dwarfs. They were midgets. They were very polite to each other.

I also knew the "Tattooed Lady." She told me that her father had started tattooing her when she was very young, with very beautiful designs — colorful butterflies, birds, and flowers. People wanted to see them, so she decided to go into the circus. She, too, wanted to lead a normal life, but she knew no other way to earn a living. The "tallest man in the world" came to our door once, and he had to walk stooped over, in our low-ceilinged house. The snake charmer was a lovely lady, and she told me confidentially that her snakes were harmless, and could not hurt anyone. She told me to feel their skin, and I was very surprised at how soft and silky they felt—not at all rough or slimy.

The other performers I didn't see much of, but I heard a great deal about them. Of all public performers, few flirt with death as often as these graceful men and women who execute miracles high in midair under the big top. The acts may vary, but the risks are always there. A split-second error in timing could result in instant death or permanent injury, whether the person is on a swaying pole, or a flying trapeze, or a thin wire.

And yet these circus daredevils are a very cautious lot. They practice constantly. They know each and every movement to the nth degree. They take no chances. They are very strict with each other, and insist on certain standards of living. They check their equipment constantly. But in spite of all this, accidents do happen. Oddly enough, it is usually while doing some very simple trick, or when they are not working at all, but merely checking on something.

My sideshow visitors told me of many such accidents. A terrible thing happened to Leitzel, a very popular entertainer who fell to her death because an iron ring cracked. "The Queen of the Air," as she was called, was mourned deeply.

They also told me about Oliver Amerika, one of

the best known and most daring of all trapeze performers, who took hold of the wrong rope, and plummeted to the ground. The audience panicked, and many children were crushed to death. They told a sad story of how Harold Adams and his sister fell from their high wire during a show in Miami, Florida, after they had done all the daring tricks and were just taking their bows.

There were many other later incidents. In Hartford, Connecticut, there was a terrible fire and many adults and children were burned to death. As my circus friends told me about this incident, the tears flowed. It was a very tragic thing, and the circus suffered from it. A combination of rumors and criticism led to the abolishment of the big top.

Many performers work far beyond usual retirement age. During World War I, they told me, Pop Otari went back to the circus to replace a boy who had to go to war. And Con Galeano was a grandfather, way past retirement age, and he was still doing somersaults on a very high thin wire, without a net. Most performers dislike a net. It may seem safer to us, but it is not. Falling the wrong way into a net could break a back or a neck, or even the ankles if they landed on their feet.

I have good reason to remember one couple who owned handsome performing dogs and horses. My son David begged to work with them, and this couple became attached to him. They bought him a uniform, and he appeared with them on stage. Before they left, they came to see me, and asked me to allow David to travel with them for the summer. His father and I refused to let him go, and he sobbed all night. I'm not sure now if we were right or wrong.

Then there was the night when David and two or three other boys in the neighborhood decided to make a little money and park cars in the backyard. They packed a hundred or more cars in the yard, and then left. When the show was over, it was a terrible mess. A near riot took place. We had to call the police. It took hours for the cars to get out, and for things to settle down. And the boys were in trouble.

The big top tent is now a thing of the past. There were too many tragic accidents. Circuses now are held in fireproof structures. But people love to talk about the old-time circuses, and to read about them. They have become endowed with a special quality of high drama. The daily dream of many a small boy was to become part of the life under the big top.

I often think of those days when I was close to the life of the circus people for a few days, and got to know some of them quite well. They were wonderful people. Though the life is hard and dangerous, they were courageous, dauntless, cheerful. They lived one day at a time, and were grateful for each day that passed without mishap.

White Elephants

THERE SHOULD BE AN ORGANIZATION CALLED "Hoarders Anonymous." I'd be the first to join. I come from a long line of hoarders. It's an inherited malady. I'm sure I got a fine start from my mother, and my grandmother was no slouch at it, either, even though their paths ran in different directions.

Mama hoarded recipes from every newspaper and magazine she could get hold of. She was a great clipper. Poems (especially Ella Wheeler Wilcox), letters to the editor, jokes, anything of interest. She never had time to file these items properly, so she stuck them behind mirrors and pictures. To move a mirror in our house was to invite a shower of clippings on your head.

She also cherished old Christmas cards, used dress patterns, embroidery designs she never had time to use, small *objets d'art,* and pretty china, even if it was nicked or cracked. Any of these things you might find hidden in umbrella stands, or deep vases, or old cookie tins. And we had more pickle dishes piled up on the sideboard than we had pickles to put in them.

Grandma's "saving graces" applied to anything that took her fancy. Christmas gifts from way back, too pretty to use; teacups without handles, too pretty to throw away; Grandpa's old silk neckties (she might decide to make a quilt someday soon), old almanacs (she loved to argue about the weather), and tintype portraits no one recognized anymore. And mountains of the grandchildren's drawings.

Then there was Aunt Matilda. She loved to tell people that she had been in the "theater" world, and it must have been so, for there was a trunk in the attic full of sequined dresses, wigs, feathery boas, long pastel stockings patterned in dots and diamonds, and gold and silver slippers. There was a large tinted photograph of Aunt Matilda, and I was very embarrassed when I first saw it, by the lack of cover above, and the show of legs below.

Aunt Matilda must have been quite a bird, though she died an "old maid" at ninety-one. She collected dance programs crammed with names like Hiram, Josh, Julius, and Jacob, and they were still in the trunk, along with paperweights from Niagara Falls, ashtrays from Fairmount Park in Philadelphia, and a fan with the words, "Meet Me in St. Louis, at the Fair."

All those things were in the attic in my childhood home. As a child I hoarded seashells of any kind, silken cigarette flags, cigar bands, and flower name cards. Every little girl had her own name card, a cutout flower of cardboard with her name printed on it. These she would exchange for other little girls' name cards, and the more you could gather, the more popular you were.

But in our home, also, we had an attic. And an attic is a hoarder's heaven. To be a hoarder and not have an attic—I can't imagine a worse catastrophe. The modern ranch-type home is functional enough, but it is no place for anyone with a yen for collecting—hoarders, that is.

If you collect old letters, string from parcels, pieces of silver foil only slightly wrinkled, rubber bands from celery, metal twists from bread wrappers, we'd be bosom pals.

I hoard magazines. I hate to get rid of one, so they pile up. But I can't match my mother's piles of *Youth's Companions*, *St. Nicholas*, *Geographics*, and *Godey's Ladies Magazine*s.

Now, in my own home I have this problem. What to do with all this accumulation? An apartment is not like a house with an attic, and my loot is getting out of hand. To get something from a shelf in my closet is something I do with bated breath. I open each drawer with a prayer. And a promise to get rid of most of its contents.

I am always captivated by auctions and "white elephant" sales at any bazaar. I'm elated if I can pick up a choice item like a sterling silver crumb scraper, even though I know they went out when placemats came in. And I can't resist that dented copper teakettle, though I know I'll never get it repaired. But such a tiny price, and such quality!

I dread bringing these things into the house, for I know I will be greeted with scorn. "More junk!" Sometimes I manage to sneak them in under my coat, but sooner or later they'll be discovered, the hiding places in my apartment being practically nil. Then I'm in disgrace again.

I notice, however, that my children are "chips off the old block." Those hecklers are not above a little hoarding themselves. My daughter collects miniature shoes from all over the world. She must have over one hundred pairs by now. Very nice too, but if it keeps on they're going to walk her right out of her home. And why does my son keep all those smelly pipes? They are no ornament in that Bristol vase on the fireplace shelf. And the old shoes in his closet must be a little green by now. And the old tires piled up in his garage; does he expect a huge rubber shortage?

Another daughter collects "salts and peppers" — shakers, that is, though I remember noticing that those on the table were not very efficient. At last count she said she had over two hundred pairs.

Another son had three suitcases filled with science fiction paperbacks, early editions. But when he found out that they were worth real money, he disposed of them quickly, thus eliminating himself from my proposed society. But he has never ceased to mourn them.

Now I see that even my grandchildren are learning very early to hoard. They collect bits of broken crayons, toy cars without wheels, windup toys that won't work anymore. Throw one out, and there's a howl when it's missed. They cherish dolls with no arms or no legs, balls that have lost their bounce, and dirty teddy bears, which you can't wash without raising a wail of anguished protest.

This proves clearly that a "Hoarders Anonymous" society is badly needed. Each one of us could give the other the moral support, stamina, and courage to dispose of all surplus items cluttering up our atmosphere. Our homes would look neat again, and we'd get lots and lots of clear spaces in our closets and on our shelves. Then, if we went to auctions or bazaars, and saw something real good, we'd have a place to put it.

A World I Never Made

SINCE I'M NINETY-FIVE YEARS OLD, IT MAY BE THAT "YOU can't teach an old dog new tricks," but I'm just not comfortable with new appliances. They make me nervous and seem to know I'm a square. They never work for me.

I had a microwave. The first time I used it to bake a potato, it exploded (the potato did), and cleaning up the oven was no fun. I still can't understand how you can cook with an oven that doesn't get hot.

You never know what is going on with the new cleaning machines. You see only a tiny red light or hear a faint bleep. I knew when my old-style vacuum cleaner was working. It went *clunk, clunk, clunk* and buzzed, so I knew something was going on there.

One of my friends has a kitchen that resembles a mad scientist's laboratory. This same friend recently "renovated" her bathroom, and I'm afraid to enter it.

Another family I know has an "entertainment center"—a television, a videocassette recorder, a projector and large screen, a stereo, and several strange machines I am not familiar with. I asked if they could play some old songs I loved. "No," they said. And every family with children must have a computer. How else could they do their homework?

I met a young mother the other day on her way to the tape rental store to get a new tape for her three-year-old Jimmie. "He's getting very bored with the one he has," she said. I thought of the records I played over and over again for my kids, and how they never tired of them.

Do children need to learn basic skills nowadays, with these modern machines ready to do anything at a minute's notice? Do they need to take cooking lessons when dinners come ready to place in a microwave oven and are ready to eat in a few minutes? I heard a child remark in a supermarket, "Look, Mom, only six minutes" as she held up a TV dinner.

As for the video recorder, I can live without it. Not long ago, I went to visit a friend I hadn't seen for a long time. She greeted me with: "Oh! You are just in time to see my new movie!" As soon as it was over, I hurried to get home because it was getting dark.

This year, my kids didn't sing "Happy Birthday" to me. They played it, while they just stood and looked at me. I didn't enjoy it at all. I guess I'm just not ready for all this.

What they should invent are bottles and jars that open at a touch. Typewriters that never need a new ribbon. Pans that won't allow anything to burn. Oh, wonderful world!

The Journey

MAMA WAS GOING TO BE A HUNDRED YEARS OLD IN December, just before Christmas 1974, and my husband and I wanted to do something very special for her birthday. What could we do? She didn't need clothes. She seldom went out. We knew she'd receive all the usual gifts—handkerchiefs, talcum powder, slippers.

"There must be something very special, you'd like, Mother," we asked her. She was sitting in her highback padded rocker, her eyes closed, slowly rocking back and forth, her long silver-gray hair in two braids like a coronet around her head. She had put a faint touch of palest pink over her cheekbones, on her smooth ivory skin. She had on a pretty flowered dress, and a tiny, dainty white apron. Can a hundred-year-old lady look pretty? Mama looked pretty. She was frail and tiny. But her deep brown eyes were alert and bright, and sparkled when she became interested. Her hearing had been failing for some time, but she could hear, she said, "if only people wouldn't mumble so." Her mind was very sharp, and she did always seem to get the drift of the conversation.

We teased her a little more. "Think hard, Mother. There must be something very special you'd like, that no one would think of." Suddenly she smiled her lovely smile. "You know," she said, "there really is! I think of it often. Do you know, I have never been back to the place of my childhood. To the home of my Grand-mère, where I visited so often. Or to the nearby church where I was married, so very young, only sixteen years old. Or to the graveyard behind the church, where all my uncles I loved are buried, and Grand-mère too. Oh! Would it be possible? If I dressed very warmly? It's not so very far, only about fifty miles, and I'd be very comfortable in the rear seat of your nice car." She laughed aloud in anticipation. "Oh! That would be a most wonderful birthday gift."

December 13 turned out to be a beautiful, bright, crisp winter day. When we arrived, just after lunch, Mother was dressed and waiting for us, wearing a long, warm cape buttoned tight around her shoulders, and boots and mittens. Against her protests, we tied a scarf over her hat, and under her chin. "I look like an old lady with that on," she said. We got her comfortable in the car, and off we went.

At first, she was very quiet. Then she started chattering. She couldn't believe we were on the right road. "It can't be," she kept repeating. "Everything has changed so. Everything is so strange." But then she would see something familiar to her. "But yes! I remember that old inn. How wonderful! It is still there. But so many tall buildings! This little town has grown so. Grand-père had a cobbler shop here. Now it is gone. Forever gone. Oh! Why must things change so? Here, there was a brook, and a covered bridge. It was so much more picturesque. Those tall buildings are ugly. Oh dear!"

It was suddenly very quiet. We looked back. Mama was asleep. "Good," we thought. "A little rest before her great adventure." About ten minutes afterwards, she started her chatter again. "Oh dear! I must have dozed. And I didn't want to miss a thing. But look! We must be almost there. I remember that roadside field. It hasn't changed. I used to pick blueberries there. Oh! What berries! As big as your thumb. Do they still grow there, I wonder?"

And on and on she chattered. "We will come to the church before we come to Grand-mère's house. Grand-mère and Grand-père had bought the house from an old Dutchman who had been a first settler in the area. I lived in Webster, but the house was in Grovsnordale. That is the way they spelled it in those days. They had six sons. My six uncles. I remember all their names. Nelson, Hector, Xavier, Napoleon, Ezra, and James, the youngest, and my favorite. Uncle Jim. I loved them all, but Uncle Jim I adored. Grand-père came from Normandy, but all the boys were born in Canada. Grand-père died quite young, in his fifties, and the boys all worked hard to keep up the small farm, and they worked in the Webster mills.

Uncle Jim always called me his little Yankee, teased me and loved me.

"I'll know the house when I see it. I've seen it in my mind's eye so often. And oh! I hope the church hasn't changed much. It was such a pretty little church. On the day of our wedding, we had filled it with field flowers. I had made my own brown silk dress and bonnet, and your Papa, oh! he was such a handsome boy, had on his first long pants, and a white linen shirt I had made him. He was only seventeen years old. He had run away from home in Canada to work in the mills in Webster. I met him at a party, and it was love at first sight."

We had heard this story many times before, but we listened. For she always had something new to add that we hadn't heard before.

"Your Papa was very clever with his hands," she went on, "and when he found out that he could earn one dollar a day, learning to mold small articles in an ironworks foundry, we moved to Worcester, right after we were married. We found a nice little three-room flat over a store, for four dollars a month, and for me, it was Paradise. It was an exciting place to live, for it was right near the Blackstone River, where barges, led by mules, went up and down the shores all day and night. That was the main way freight was transported in those days. I could run out to a barge which was unloading and buy a big bag of potatoes, or other produce, very cheap."

Suddenly, she became very excited. "Why look!"

she exclaimed. "How wonderful! We are here! Really here! Stop! This is the church. It has been enlarged. But it hasn't changed so very much. Oh! How wonderful! I am really here. I can't believe it."

We helped her from the car, and into the church. She patted each pew lovingly. Her eyes filled with tears, but she was smiling. "Look! That is where we stood when he put the ring on my finger." She looked down at the ring, still shining brightly there on her finger, then lifted it to her lips and kissed it. "My dear sweet boy husband."

We led her through the rear door of the church into the graveyard. We made her sit on a bench while we searched, and finally found them, all together, eight small gravestones. Then we brought her to them. The tears were streaming down her face, but again, she was smiling. She rested her hand on each stone, and spoke each name tenderly. "Dear beloved uncles. I hope to see you soon." But when she came to Uncle Jim's stone, she wept a little. "Dear Uncle Jim. I hope you knew how much I loved you." Then she turned away. "Come, now. I want to see Grand-mère's house while the sun is shining."

We got her settled in the car again and rode on. After a few moments of silence, she started to chatter again. "Oh! Everything has changed so. but the terrain is the same. There is the hill where the little brick schoolhouse was. All gone now. And look! There is the little depot where the train stopped to let me off when I came to visit. Why, we must be here. Stop the car, please. But this can't be Grand-mère's house. It can't be. Yet, there is where the well sweep was. And there is where the big tree was, that held the rope swing on a thick branch. Oh! How Uncle Jim pushed me right up into the clouds." Mama was very excited now. "We must find out about the house," she said.

I stepped from the car and knocked at the door. A stout woman with iron gray hair opened it. She didn't seem to speak or understand English very well, and I had difficulty making her understand what I wanted. But after a while I got the message to her, and then she was very friendly and kind.

Yes, it was the same house, but a wing had been added, and it had been shingled over with asbestos shingles. She had bought it from the last living member of a family who had lived there for many years. That must have been Uncle Jim. She invited us in. "Oh yes! Bring her in, bring her in," she said in broken English. Her name was Natalie, she said, and she was Polish.

We brought Mama in from the car, after we convinced her that this was indeed Grand-mère's house. We introduced the ladies. "Natalie, this is Roseanne." They embraced. "How kind of you, how very kind, to invite me in," Mama said. And once she was inside, she recognized all the familiar things.

"The same fireplace. But the books are gone. Here is where I first learned to read. There were six books on that shelf over the fireplace. I still remember the titles. *Aesop's Fables,* the Bible, *Darkest Africa* with horrible illustrations that frightened me. *Milestones*, a very large book of stories and poems, many of which I learned by heart. One of which, 'Spartacus to the Gladiators,' I can recite most of to this day. And two books in French which Uncle Jim tried, in vain, to teach me to read."

"You must have a cup of tea, now," said Natalie, and she busied herself with cups and saucers while Mama looked around, so happy to find many things "just as they used to be." We excused ourselves and stepped out to walk in the yard, to allow the ladies to enjoy their tea and conversation. Mama could speak a little Polish, and they seemed to understand and enjoy each other.

After an hour or so, we came in to bring her back to the car. Mama and Natalie kissed, and Mama said, over and over, "Oh! Thank you, thank you. It is like a dream. You have been so kind."

She was very quiet all the way home. It was getting dark. We got her into bed. "I am very, very tired," she said. "But oh—so happy. What a wonderful day. A beautiful day. I've thought of it so often. Now, I can die happy. Thank you, dear, dear children. I want to be alone now, to rest, and to think." And a small hand reached out to us.

P.S. But Mama didn't die right away. She lived, with tender, loving care, for more than six years after the journey. She died in her sleep, peacefully, naturally, without pain.

Smiling.

People Making A Difference

Family Bookshelf offers the finest in good wholesome Christian literature, written by best-selling authors. All books are recommended by an Advisory Board of distinguished writers and editors.

We are also a vital part of a compassionate outreach called **Bowery Mission Ministries**. Our evangelical mission is devoted to helping the destitute of the inner city.

Our ministries date back more than a century and began by aiding homeless men lost in alcoholism. Now we also offer hope and Gospel strength to homeless, inner-city women and children. Our goal, in fact, is to end homelessness by teaching these deprived people how to be independent with the Lord by their side.

Downtrodden, homeless men are fed and clothed and may enter a discipleship program of one-on-one professional counseling, nutrition therapy and Bible study. This same Christian care is provided at our women and children's shelter.

We also welcome nearly 1,000 underprivileged children each summer at our Mont Lawn Camp located in Pennsylvania's beautiful Poconos. Here, impoverished youngsters enjoy the serenity of nature and an opportunity to receive the teachings of Jesus Christ. We also provide year-round assistance through teen activities, tutoring in reading and writing, Bible study, family counseling, college scholarships and vocational training.

During the spring, fall and winter months, our children's camp becomes a lovely retreat for religious gatherings of up to 200. Excellent accommodations include heated cabins, chapel, country-style meals and recreational facilities. Write to Paradise Lake Retreat Center, Box 252, Bushkill, PA 18324 or call: (717) 588-6067.

Still another vital part of our ministry is **Christian Herald magazine**. Our dynamic, bimonthly publication focuses on the true personal stories of men and women who, as "doers of the Word," are making a difference in their lives and the lives of others.

Bowery Mission Ministries are supported by voluntary contributions of individuals and bequests. Contributions are tax deductible. Checks should be made payable to Bowery Mission.

 Fully accredited Member
of the Evangelical Council
for Financial Accountability

Every Monday morning, our ministries staff joins together in prayer. If you have a prayer request for yourself or a loved one, simply write to us.

 Administrative Office:
40 Overlook Drive, Chappaqua,
New York 10514 Telephone: (914) 769-9000